A Sociological Yearbook of Religion in Britain 7

JMacwar :.
- 199x -

A Sociological Yearbook
of Religion in Britain · 7

Edited by Michael Hill

SCM PRESS LTD

334 01594 4

First published 1974
by SCM Press Ltd
56 Bloomsbury Street London WC1

© SCM Press Ltd 1974

Printed in Great Britain by
Northumberland Press Ltd, Gateshead

CONTENTS

The Contributors   vii

Preface   ix

1 British Theology as a Sociological Variable   1
  Robin Gill

2 Participation, Reform and Ecumenism: The Views of   13
  Laity and Clergy
  Alan Bryman and C. Robin Hinings

3 The Nature of Religion in Ireland   26
  Malcolm Macourt

4 The Great Yorkshire Revival 1792-6: A Study of   46
  Mass Revival among the Methodists
  John Baxter

5 Making Sense and Meaning: A Documentary Method   77
  of Analysis
  Ross McLeod

6 Social Change and the Church of Scotland   91
  Madeleine Maxwell-Arnot

7 Seventh-day Adventists and the Millennium   111
  Robin Theobald

8 The Swedenborgians: An Interactionist Analysis   132
  Robert Kenneth Jones

9 Bibliography of Work in the Sociology of British   154
  Religion, 1973 Supplement
  Ronald Iphofen and James Edmiston

THE CONTRIBUTORS

JOHN BAXTER   Postgraduate Student, The Department of Economic History, University of Sheffield

ALAN BRYMAN   Research Fellow, Institute for the Study of Worship and Religious Architecture, University of Birmingham

JAMES EDMISTON   Graduate Student, University of York

ROBIN GILL   Lecturer in the Sociology of Religion, Department of Christian Ethics and Practical Theology, University of Edinburgh

C. ROBIN HININGS   Senior Research Fellow, Institute of Local Government Studies, University of Birmingham

RONALD IPHOFEN   Graduate Student, University of York

ROBERT KENNETH JONES   Staff Tutor in Sociology, Faculty of Social Science, Open University, North West of England

MALCOLM MACOURT   Fellow in Social Statistics, North-East Area of Study, University of Durham; previously Lecturer in Statistics, University of Dundee

MADELEINE MAXWELL-ARNOT   Research Student, Institute of Education, University of London

ROSS MCLEOD   Research Assistant and Tutor, Department of Sociology, University of Leeds

ROBIN THEOBALD   Lecturer in Sociology, Polytechnic of Central London

PREFACE

Like the previous editions, Yearbook number seven follows a broad editorial policy, with a mixture of contemporary and historical, theoretical and empirical articles. One of the most rewarding aspects of editing a collection of this kind is the wealth of excellent material which is now being produced. The sociology of religion is clearly in great shape and is served by some first-rate British contributors (a claim which I do not mind making this year, since I am not one of them).

Robin Gill's opening paper makes an important demand for sociologists to take theology more seriously. As he observes, the pioneering work of Max Weber gave a central place to theological statements, as for example in his germinal study of the rise of Western capitalism. Since much of the recent growth in the sociological study of religion has been brought about by a rediscovery of its roots in classical sociology, we may hope that a more perceptive treatment of theology will emerge as part of this rediscovery. On the whole – and with notable exceptions such as Peter Berger – sociologists have been hampered in their treatment of theology by a 'Muggeridge syndrome', by the tendency to view theology as a fixed, definitive, archaic and above all other-worldly body of assertions. At the same time it must also be pointed out that some contemporary theologians who have used sociological insights in their work have tended on their part to rely on a crude global optimism drawn from Comte rather than from the more agnostic and pessimistic outlook of the Weberian tradition. There is thus room for *détente* on both sides, and it will only be achieved if sociologists and theologians agree that there exists between them a division of labour rather than a conflict of interests. There is splendid confirmation of a possible *rapport* between theology and sociology in the statement that '... whatever processes of growth in Christian or Catholic ideas and institutions may be revealed by history as explicable by sociological or psychological laws, it does

not follow that they are corruptions or perversions of the gospel
ideas proclaimed by Christ, so long as these ideas live and work on
throughout the course of the development'. Those are not the words
of a sociologist (though their relevance for the Weberian concept
of 'routinization' will be immediately apparent) but of a prominent
Catholic theologian, Dom Cuthbert Butler. They deserve the *nihil
obstat* of sociology.

The article by Gill begins by exploring three possible models
which concern the interaction between theology and sociology and
opts for one which permits the analysis of theology as an autonomous variable. Having established this perspective, he goes on to
provide a sociological interpretation of the *Honest to God* debate
and the breakdown of the Anglican/Methodist union scheme in
1969. His argument for an interdisciplinary approach is cogent and
stimulating and should evoke a response.

Another view of the ecumenical movement is given in the
following article by Alan Bryman and Bob Hinings, who compare
the attitudes to church authority and unity of clergy and laity in
an Anglican diocese. The laity, it seems, rank themselves only
slightly more influential in church affairs than assistant curates,
while the clergy see the laity as having almost as much influence
as incumbents. This study confirms with great precision the sub-
stantially higher proportion of clergy as against laity who are in
favour of church unity. On specific forms of ecumenical venture,
however – for instance, the sharing of churches, services and theological colleges – there was little significant difference between
clergy and laity.

Malcolm Macourt's article follows the tradition of the religious
demographers Horace Mann and Abraham Hume by considering
data on religious allegiance in the Irish Census of Population. The
article distinguishes between religious groupings and tribal groupings, traces some of the effects of partition on the religious situation
of the Republic and the North, and succeeds in shedding important
light on the religious dimensions of the present conflict. The introduction of historical data into the discussion helps to locate it
against the background of Ireland's mixed religious pedigree.

A different historical controversy provides the theme of John
Baxter's article on the revival of 1792-6 among the Yorkshire
Methodists. This article takes up a debate which has in recent
years attracted a great deal of attention on the part of sociologists

(largely, one suspects, because of its treatment by E. P. Thompson and Eric Hobsbawm): was Methodism an agent of counter-revolution in the later part of the eighteenth and early nineteenth century? Baxter finds excellent evidence in his study of the Yorkshire revival to support Thompson's contention that Methodism was such an agent and his careful research provides an effective counterblast to the views of Currie and Hartwell who, he suggests, seem almost unaware of the existence of popular radical activity. This article contributes a valuable case study to the literature on 'the Halévy thesis'.

The last Yearbook contained an article on 'common religion' which attempted to explore new research strategies in the sociological interpretation of contemporary religion. This one contains another piece of research which taps the non-institutional components of belief systems and offers a documentary method of analysing the systems of meaning used by actors in a situation. Ross McLeod's paper is very much a new departure and represents a genuine attempt to use a sociology of knowledge perspective which spans both popular religion and social movements in a broader sense. His analysis of the way in which a cluster of values and strategies is built up by supporters of Women's Liberation contains a clear blueprint for the use of similar research procedures in the study of religion. Research in this field, incidentally, seems to represent another kind of 'Yorkshire revival' because much of the empirical work centres on the University of Leeds.

Religion in Scotland presents a number of striking contrasts with the religious situation in the rest of Great Britain, yet it has been very little studied by sociologists of religion. Previous editions of the Yearbook have, however, contained articles on some of the more interesting recent pieces of research on religion in Scotland. Madeleine Maxwell-Arnot's contribution is based on a large-scale statistical study of organizational change and ministerial recruitment in the Church of Scotland. She traces the gradual decline of traditional social and geographical areas of recruitment and, by employing categories which have been used in studying recruitment of clergy to the Church of England, she provides a firm basis for comparison. Different as the religious culture of Scotland may be, the problems faced by its religious institutions are by no means unique and might benefit from such comparative work.

Another problem of religious organization is faced by groups which prophesy a millennium which fails to materialize. This happened during the early history of the group now known as the Seventh-day Adventists, and Robin Theobald shows how the branches of the movement reinterpreted the original prophecy of William Miller. The movement is presented as a complex synthesis of intellectualism and emotionalism, of social protest and social mobility. Theobald's treatment is a valuable corrective to an over-simplified approach to millenarian religion.

Little has been written from either a sociological or a historical viewpoint on the Swedenborgians, and the article by Ken Jones sets about tracing the background, history and beliefs of the group. His interactionist analysis shows how a religious body whose beliefs are at variance with those prevailing in the wider society is able to maintain its divergent ideology. Mechanisms such as social insulation are ways of reinforcing the plausibility structure of groups like this.

Finally, we must once again express our enormous debt to the compilers of the 1973 Supplement to the Bibliography. It will greatly assist them if researchers would keep us informed of their work, and as always we welcome general comments and suggestions on the Yearbook.

The London School of Economics   MICHAEL HILL
& Political Science

1 British Theology as a Sociological Variable

Robin Gill

Sociologists have seldom taken theology very seriously. Of course, there was a time when they ignored religion too, notably in the thirty years between 1920 and 1950. Before the 1920s it was respectable, and some of the most important pioneers of socio-logical enquiry wrote at length about religion. Today, too, the sociology of religion is once again a respectable pursuit for the sociologist, either in America or in Britain. Currently it is no longer religion which is ignored but theology.

There are probably several reasons why theology is ignored by the sociologist. The first is surely a language barrier between the two disciplines. Confronting a theologian with Talcott Parsons or a sociologist with Paul Tillich is hardly likely to lead to a fruitful inter-change of ideas: both disciplines confront the non-specialist with a welter of words and half-explained labels that effectively block communication. But secondly, sociologists may be inclined to consider that theology is frankly irrelevant – irrelevant, that is, as a significant religious variable. The theologian still has a reputation in some circles for arguing endlessly about whether or not God could move an immovable stone, or about how many angels could sit on the end of a pin! It is possible that profes-sional theorists in any field are always in danger of becoming removed from popular feelings, beliefs and experiences. Finally, it should be pointed out that theologians themselves may not be too keen on an inspection of theology by sociologists. The socio-logist still has a reputation in some quarters for wishing to 'explain away' religion.

Whatever the reasons for this neglect of theology by sociologists, the proposition that theology *is* relevant to the sociology of religion should at least be considered seriously. It is after all the job of the sociologist to relate values to actions and theories to practice.

Further, the great pioneer of contemporary sociology, Max Weber, was clearly undaunted by the difficulties that theology presents to the sociologist. His *The Protestant Ethic and the 'Spirit' of Capitalism* (1905) was perhaps the first and the last significant attempt by a sociologist to take theology seriously. The time may be ripe for another, though no doubt less ambitious, attempt of this kind to be made.

This paper will fall into three parts. In the first I will explore three possible models concerned with an interaction between theology and sociology, and will opt for the more specifically sociological of the three. In the second I will examine two case-studies drawn from the theology of the 1960s. During this time it is arguable that British theology was dominated by at least two themes, the problem of secularization and the issue of ecumenism. Accordingly, my first case-study will centre upon the *Honest to God* (1963) debate: whereas the second will concentrate upon the breakdown of the proposed Anglican/Methodist Union in 1969. The controversial nature of the subject matter of both of these case-studies makes them ideal hunting ground for the sociologist. In the final part I will attempt to draw some theoretical conclusions about the relevance of British theology for the sociologist of religion in Britain today.

I

Just because the frontiers between theology and sociology have seldom been explored, it is important to suggest a number of ways such a venture is possible. The following three models are not, of course, intended to be exhaustive.

1. *A sociology of theological positions*

This approach would involve a specific examination of theologians from the sociological perspective, in an attempt to see how they had been influenced by society at large. It is clear that theologians do not work in a vacuum: inevitably they are influenced by others. So it is possible that the sociologist could perform a useful task in analysing, for example, the effect of the last war on Karl Barth and on neo-orthodox theology in general.

In an important appendix to his *The Social Reality of Religion* Peter Berger outlines such an approach when he argues that sociology 'raises questions for the theologian to the extent that the latter's positions hinge on certain socio-historical presuppositions ... such presuppositions are particularly characteristic of theological thought in the Judaeo-Christian orbit.' Further, sociology becomes relevant as soon as the theologian 'reflects that, after all, he was not born as a theologian, that he existed as a person in a particular socio-historical situation before he ever began to do theology'.[1]

2. *A sociology of the theological situation*

This approach shifts attention away from the theologian to theology itself, calling for a sociological analysis of contemporary 'plausibility structures' in the belief that these are relevant to theology. Again, Berger has written at length about the relation between plausibility structures and religious thinking.[2] Plausibility structures involve our most basic presuppositions about reality: they are the very ways in which we verify things. Sociologists usually argue that the way we verify things varies from age to age and from society to society. Clearly it is important for the theologian to know something about how people think and about how they identify 'objective reality', especially if he is to communicate with others. So it follows that the sociologist could assist the theologian by uncovering for him the social context within which his theology is to operate.

Both of these models are theologically oriented. That is to say, although they require someone with sociological training to perform them, the goods that they may produce will probably be of greater interest to the theologian than the sociologist. In this sense they may properly belong to 'religious sociology' rather than the 'sociology of religion'. Nevertheless, they do avoid the danger of jumping too quickly from sociological descriptions to theological prescriptions. Harvey Cox's *The Secular City*[3] well illustrates this danger. Cox started from a purely sociological analysis of the city, believing (perhaps wrongly) that 'anonymity' and 'pragmatism' were central characteristics of the city. However, he quickly moved from this descriptive level to that of theological prescriptions, arguing that 'anonymity' and 'pragmatism' were essentially providential and accorded with the Bible. The jump here is from the 'is' to the 'ought': even if 'anonymity' and 'pragmatism' were characteristics of a city the theologian would still have to decide on independent grounds whether or not these characteristics were in accord with the will of God. It is possible that even Peter Rudge's[4] brilliant application of Weber's organizational theories to the churches faces the same problem, since he jumps from a sociological analysis of the churches in these terms to a theological justification of certain organizational patterns.

3. *Theological positions as sociological variables*

It is this final approach which is most directly relevant to the sociology of religion as distinct from religious sociology. This approach takes seriously the possibility that theology may exert an influence on, rather than just be influenced by, others. Weber's genuinely interactionist approach to sociology allowed him to suggest that religion could both be influenced by and be an influence upon society at large. Whereas Durkheim viewed the influence of religion as little more than a bolster to the *status quo*, Weber took a more radical view of the role of religion within society. Further, in the specific instance of Calvinism he attempted to trace an interaction between theological ideas and society at large. Whatever the merits of Weber's particular thesis (either from the sociological or theological perspective), it *was* an attempt to take theology seriously as a sociological variable. For Weber theology was one of the complex series of variables that must be considered, not just within the sociology of religion, but within sociology as a whole. However, even the more limited claim that theology is relevant as a variable to the sociology of religion, would be worth establishing.

It is just this final point that I wish to pursue in this paper. In terms of a question it is as follows: Does theology exert any influence on general religiousness within Britain today?

II

Of course, an exhaustive answer to this question is not possible here. Instead I can only outline two case-studies: these at least can point to possibilities which a more lengthy study might uncover.

Case-study 1. *Honest to God*

John Robinson's *Honest to God*[5] makes a particularly good case-study in the present context for several reasons. In the first place it had a fairly traumatic effect on contemporary theology: few writers in theology failed to mention it, if only to refute it. It was reviewed widely and led swiftly to the publication of *The Honest to God Debate*.[6] The Archbishop of Canterbury immediately produced a critical pamphlet entitled *Images Old and New*[7], though a few years later he could write more soberly:

> Since the stirring of the theological waters some five years ago by Bishop John Robinson's *Honest to God*, theology in England has to a large extent lost what we can now see to have been a long-established insularity. It was perhaps that insularity which made some of us slow to grasp what was happening. It was not that some people called 'new theologians' were inventing theologies of compromise with the secular world: it was rather that they were to trying to meet, often in clumsy and muddled ways, pressures and currents already moving powerfully in and beyond Christendom.[8]

This quotation is particularly interesting since it indicates that despite the oft-repeated claim that *Honest to God* said nothing new, at least some people within the church thought that it had made a considerable impression on theology.

In the second place, *Honest to God* makes a good case-study because its impact extended far beyond theological circles. The Archbishop of Canterbury publicly criticized Robinson on television; a flood of letters appeared in the national newspapers: And Robinson himself wrote articles in *The Observer*, *The Sunday Mirror*, *The Sun*, *Tit-Bits* and *TV Times*. Finally, it should be pointed out that *Honest to God*, of course, became a 'best-seller': an unusual characteristic of contemporary theological works.

The combination of these three features of *Honest to God*—its traumatic effect on theologians, its creation of interest outside theological circles and its status as a 'best-seller'—must count as fairly strong *a priori* evidence that it did influence general religiousness during the mid-1960s. Nevertheless, the question must still be raised about the exact nature of this possible influence.

The contents of *Honest to God* naturally fall under four headings—God, Christ, Prayer and Morality. Under the first heading Robinson examined 'images' of God. With liberal quotations from the three theologians Tillich, Bonhoeffer and Bultmann, he suggested that we must break away from traditional theism and from notions of God as 'a Being' or as 'out there', and start theology instead from notions of God as 'ultimate reality', 'Being' or 'the Ground of our Being', substituting images of depth for those of height. Under the second heading Robinson rejected the image that Christ 'came down to earth' from the Father, or the notion that he was not '*a* man': instead he suggested that Jesus as a man was completely united to 'the Ground of his Being'. Under the third heading he rejected the notion of worship as 'withdrawal' from the world, and under the last, despite the provocative title, 'The New Morality', he advanced a fairly traditional morality, though one which was not 'God-given' and unchangeable.

Baldly summarized in this way the contents of *Honest to God* may not appear to be too remarkable. Further, Robinson's heavy dependence on Tillich, Bonhoeffer and Bultmann (none of whom present easy reading for the non-theologian) and his use of un-explained theological jargon (such as the concept of 'Being' or the phrase *deus ex machina*) create a paradox. *Honest to God* sold widely amongst non-theologians and yet it must have been unintelligible to them. Many of the letters in *The Honest to God Debate* seem to confirm this impression. In fact, Robinson himself later claimed that he did not anticipate a 'best-seller':

> The publicity explosion was neither sought nor expected. If there had been a desire to exploit the market, (a) I should not have given the manuscript to a religious publisher, (b) there would have been a special publicity-campaign to launch it, and (c) I should have written a very different book.[9]

Later, with the publication of *But that I can't Believe!*[10] Robinson indeed proved that he could write a very different book, though strangely it did not become a 'best-seller'.

So, despite the *a priori* possibility based on the trauma and publicity outside theological circles that *Honest to God* created, it may not after all have greatly influenced general religiousness. Its unintelligibility at the popular level might have precluded it from doing so.

However, this judgment ignores four non-theological features of *Honest to God* which are both intelligible at the popular level and of peculiar interest to the sociologist. It is possible that the main impact of *Honest to God* lay in them rather than in its specific theological content. Further, they help to explain why the book ever became a 'best-seller' – a point that the sociologist cannot afford to ignore.

Firstly, Robinson made great play of his function as a bishop in *Honest to God*. 'It belongs to the office of a bishop ...' were the opening words of the preface. In the first chapter he claimed that 'as a bishop I could happily get on with most of my work without ever being forced to discuss such questions' (p.18): at the end of the chapter he wrote that he was 'deliberately writing as an ordinary churchman' (p.27). From a publicity point-of-view the fact that the writer of *Honest to God* was a bishop was crucial: all clergy are vulnerable to publicity and bishops even more so. At the same time that Robinson was writing, the American Bishop Pike was causing an immense stir, and soon afterwards the national newspapers were widely reporting the facts that the Bishop of Munich was suspected of war crimes, the Bishop of Southwell had apparently eloped, the Bishop of Leicester had signed a 'keep the cricket tour' plea, and the Bishop of Coventry had condemned pornography.

Secondly, Robinson suggested on more than one occasion that what he was writing in *Honest to God* would be regarded by many as 'heretical'. The labels 'heretic' and 'atheist' occur in several parts of the book. At the end of the preface he wrote that 'what I have tried to say, in a tentative and exploratory way, may seem to be radical, and doubtless to many heretical' (p.10). In the section on God he admitted that what he had to say on the subject would be 'resisted as a denial of the Gospel by ninety per cent of the people' (p.18): in the section on morality he claimed that his views were not 'what men expect the Church to stand for' and would be 'regarded as profoundly shocking' (p.109): and in the last chapter he stated that some would think that he had 'abandoned the Christian faith and practice altogether' (p.123). The general effect of hinting so often that what one says may be 'heresy' or even 'atheism' to many, is to give the book both a provocative and an elitist nature. By insisting that the majority of people have got things wrong, an author must inevitably expect his readers to feel either angry or deprived.

Thirdly, *Honest to God* is thoroughly iconoclastic. Each of the four sections of the book begins with a demolition of traditional images: in fact it is not until page forty-four of the first section that Robinson introduces his new images for God. It is possible that this feature too confirms the provocative and elitist nature of the work.

Finally, *Honest to God* contains a surprising amount of caricature. The 'God out there' is compared with the 'old man in the sky': the traditional image of Christ is compared with an 'astro-naut': traditional prayers are called 'spiritual refills': traditional morality is said to 'come direct from heaven'. Inevitably these caricatures – and Robinson frequently admitted that they were caricatures – angered his critics. Despite the technical language of other parts of the book, they give it a quotable, and at the same time sensational, aspect.

It is possible that it is at the level of these four features – emphasis on episcopacy, hint of 'heresy', iconoclasm and caricature – that the main influence of *Honest to God* must be located. On *a priori* grounds it seems reasonable to suppose that the book did act as an important variable *vis à vis* general religious conscious-ness in Britain during the late 1960s. But on internal grounds it seems doubtful whether the contents of the book were intelligible at the popular level. However, at the non-theological level it seems possible indeed that the public experience of a bishop criticizing and caricaturing traditional Christianity and hinting that he might appear to be a 'heretic' or even an 'atheist', may well have been sociologically significant.

Case-study 2. Anglican/Methodist Union Scheme

An examination of the breakdown of the proposals for Anglican/ Methodist Union in 1969 presents different problems for the sociologist. Superficially, at least, it appears that there *was* a significant theological variable involved in this breakdown. Although the Methodists exceeded the required 75% vote in favour of the Union Scheme, as did the Church of England bishops, the Anglican clergy vote was only 69% in favour. In certain dioceses, notably London, only a bare majority of the clergy voted in favour of the Scheme. It appeared that those who voted against it divided into two camps, the Evangelicals and the Anglo-Catholics, united in the belief that the issue of episcopal ordination caused them to vote in this way. The Evangelicals, on the one hand, argued that the Methodists did not require to be ordained by a bishop since their existing orders were perfectly valid: the Anglo-Catholics, on the other, argued that the proposed re-union service did not make explicit that the Methodists were being episcopally ordained, and that unless this were to be made explicit their orders would remain invalid. Ostensibly, then, the theological issue of episcopal ordination and the validity of Methodist orders did lie at the heart of the 1969 breakdown.

However, few sociologists of religion who have considered ecumenism have allowed for theology acting as a sociological variable in this way. Bryan Turner[11] has isolated three sociological explanations of ecumenism, none of which suggests that theology plays a determinative role – namely, secularization, bureaucratization and homogenization. The first argues that the ecumenical movement is itself a feature of the process of secularization: the second tends to use a market analogy, suggesting that churches combine to appeal to a religious market in a situation where they are generally losing social significance: the third argues that ethnic, social class and cultural differences created different denominations, and that since these differences are waning in contemporary society differences between denominations become increasingly irrelevant.

Bryan Wilson tends to combine the first two of these explanations:

> Organizations amalgamate when they are weak rather than when they are strong, since alliance means compromise and amendment of commitment.[12]

For Wilson, ecumenism, far from being a sign of strength and religious 'progress', is an indication that religious practice, institutions and thinking are becoming increasingly epiphenomenal. Ecumenism is one sign amongst others that religion is no longer at the centre of the life of Western society. At no point in his analysis does he interpret the ecumenical movement as being a product, or even a partial product, of the ecumenical thinking of contemporary theologians. Whereas the latter might interpret the movement as a 'return to the gospel', or as an 'expression of Jesus' command for unity', Wilson interprets it as a manifestation of the fact that institutions only combine in times of weakness when their values are marginal and their resources low. In fact, he sees ecumenical theology itself amongst the clergy as a product of organizational weakness, that is, as a 'new faith' at a time when theology in general is weak. Theology is not a variable itself, but simply the product of other variables.

It is clear that both the secularization and the bureaucratization explanations of ecumenism are dependent on a situation of declining churches. Granted that there is a process of secularization apparent within a particular society, or at least a process of the decline of institutional churches, these explanations become viable. The third explanation instead is dependent on an increasing socio-cultural consensus within a particular society. Unfortunately, as Turner points out, it is extraordinarily difficult to get reliable evidence about any such consensus within a specific society. Just as the theory of secularization has been attacked as a meaningless and unverifiable generalization, so too socio-cultural consensus theories can be attacked in the same way. Perhaps only the decline of the institutional churches can be mapped out in any empirical fashion.

It is just at this point that the 1969 breakdown becomes interesting. Wilson and others have quite ably shown that both the Methodist Church and the Church of England have declined fairly rapidly during the course of this century. In terms of membership and participation it seems that only the Roman Catholic Church in Britain and possibly some of the smaller religious organizations have either increased or kept moderately stable. In almost every aspect the Church of England has declined, and not least in its number of ordinands. The problem of whether or not this is to be interpreted in terms of a process of secularization can be ignored in this context. It is sufficient to admit that both the Methodist Church and the Church of England are now considerably weakened organizations. Once this is admitted the 1969 breakdown becomes difficult to interpret simply in terms of a market or amalgamation model. In the absence of other variables one would confidently expect the Anglican clergy in 1969 to have voted resoundingly in favour of the Union Scheme.

The fact that they did not do so opens again the possibility that theology acted as a significant variable in this context too. It is possible that an adequate sociological account of the 1969 break-down would have to give more serious consideration than is currently apparent to the influence of theology in ecumenism.

III

The two case-studies have not claimed to be exhaustive, but simply to have pointed to a possibility – namely, that British theology should be given serious consideration as a sociological variable. Further research is clearly needed if it is to be transformed into anything more than a possibility. At present, however, it is research which is conspicuously lacking from the sociology of religion.

On the rare occasions that sociologists of religion have given serious consideration to theology, the results have not always been too satisfactory. So, for example, the sociologist J. M. Yinger[13] derived his definition of 'religion' from Paul Tillich's notion of 'ultimate concern'. The resulting functionalist definition of 'religion' may well be unsatisfactory for both the sociologist and the theologian. The sociologist Betty Scharf argues that 'it is cast in wide terms which allow almost any kind of enthusiastic purpose or strong loyalty, provided it is shared by a group, to count as religion'.[14] in similar terms the philosopher H. D. Lewis claims that 'the only way in which we could make Tillich's statement plausible would be by identifying belief in God with seriousness'.[15]

In arguing for a more sophisticated, and more thoroughly sociological, approach to theology, in terms of considering the possibility that theology may at times act as a sociological variable, my approach might be seen as a part of what Robertson and Campbell term 'co-ordinated eclecticism'. They argue strongly for 'the simultaneous deployment of a variety of methodological approaches' within the sociology of religion:

> What is now needed, and certainly not only in the case of British society, is a research stance of an open-ended kind, based on the idea that we really know very little about the 'inner-layers' of religious belief and experience.[16]

It is just at the level of these 'inner-layers' of religious belief and experience that theology may have significance. A superficial account of general religiousness no doubt can afford to ignore the possibility that theology may act as a significant variable. However, my two case-studies may serve to open the possibility that a serious account of general religiousness in the 1960s cannot afford to ignore theology in this way. Doubtless, though, as was the case with Weber, any possible interaction between theology and general religiousness will prove extraordinarily difficult to unravel.

NOTES

1. Peter L. Berger, *The Social Reality of Religion*, Faber 1969; Penguin Books 1973, pp.184-5.
2. Peter L. Berger, *A Rumour of Angels*, Penguin Books 1969.
3. Harvey Cox, *The Secular City*, SCM Press 1965.

4. Peter F. Rudge, *Ministry and Management*, Tavistock Publications 1968.

5. John A. T. Robinson, *Honest to God*, SCM Press 1963.

6. David L. Edwards and John A. T. Robinson (eds), *The Honest to God Debate*, SCM Press 1963.

7. A. M. Ramsey, *Images Old and New*, SPCK 1963.

8. A. M. Ramsey, *God, Christ and the World*, SCM Press 1969.

9. *The Honest to God Debate*, p.233.

10. John A. T. Robinson, *But that I can't Believe!*, Collins Fontana Books 1967.

11. Bryan S. Turner, 'The Sociological Explanation of Ecumenicalism', *The Social Sciences and the Churches*, ed. C. L. Mitton, T. & T. Clark 1972.

12. Bryan Wilson, *Religion in Secular Society*, Penguin Books 1966, p.152.

13. J. M. Yinger, *Religion, Society and the Individual*, Macmillan, NY 1957.

14. Betty R. Scharf, *The Sociological Study of Religion*, Hutchinson University Library 1970, p.33.

15. H. D. Lewis, *Teach yourself Philosophy of Religion*, EUP 1965, p.127.

16. R. Robertson and C. Campbell, 'Religion in Britain: the Need for New Research Strategies', *Social Compass* XIX/2, 1972, p.197.

2 Participation, Reform and Ecumenism: The Views of Laity and Clergy[1]

Alan Bryman and C. Robin Hinings

Introduction

In recent years sociologists of religion have witnessed the gradual emergence of a considerable literature concerned with the ways in which clergy and laity differ in their attitudes towards a variety of issues, religious and otherwise, and the situation of the two groups within the churches.[2] There have been two main thrusts to this work which are of interest from both a sociological and a religious standpoint. On the one hand there has been a concern to analyse the ecumenical movement. From a sociological viewpoint, the conditions under which organizations come together and new social movements launched are important. From a religious point of view the ecumenical movement is one of the most important ventures of the recent past. Hand in hand with a concern over ecumenism has gone one for reform of the structure of churches. Indeed, the two are linked, for much ecumenical co-operation, and certainly organic union, requires structural reform. Again sociologists are interested in reform movements and attitudes to reform, and this has been a concern of those active in the churches for some time past.

In this paper we hope to contribute to these two areas by examining the views of clergy and laity towards ecumenical activity and in their proclivity towards reform in the church. However, to understand the ways in which any groups perceive issues important to the organizations of which they are members one needs to examine a number of components of their organizational positions. On ecumenism, for example, Bryan Wilson has written:

... it is the religious professionals who will hold the conversations and make the recommendations, and it is largely they who will frame and vote on the resolutions on unity, even in movements which, like Methodism, have a rather strong lay tradition. Certainly it is they who will make propaganda for union and whose visits and interchanges will receive the endorsements of publicity by mass media.[3]

In addition, there is some evidence to suggest that the clergy actually resent the laity becoming involved in ecumenical matters on the grounds that the issues are too complicated for them.[4] On the question of the implementation of policies, whether concerned with ecumenism or with reform, Harrison in his study of the American Baptist Convention has pointed to the position of permanent officials.[5] This is important in voluntary organizations, similar evidence coming from Lipset, Trow and Coleman's study of the International Typographical Union.[6] Underlying this is the idea that access to, and control of organizational information may be, as Pettigrew suggests, an important power resource.[7] It is the religious professionals, the full time members, who have the greatest access to information and the possibility of controlling its flow.

This suggests that one should take account of the place of laity and clergy in the power structure of a church in accounting for differences in views between the two groups on various issues. In other words, we are suggesting that the categories of clergy and laity define positions in an organization. If one examines views on issues which are important to the organization, as are ecumenism and reform, then one needs to examine other aspects of organizational position that may influence attitudes. To this end, this paper also examines the extent of lay participation in diocesan affairs and the views of clergy and laity on the distribution of influence in the diocese.

Sampling and Procedures

The data were collected from clergy and laity in an urban Anglican diocese. The laity data are derived from a questionnaire sent to a sample of lay members of deanery synods, i.e. the lay parish representatives at the level of the rural deanery. There are thirteen rural deaneries in the diocese, only one of which refused to co-operate. Names and addresses were obtained from synod secretaries and after a pilot survey questionnaires were posted to 310 lay members of 12 deanery synods, this being a 50% sample; that is, half the lay members of each deanery synod were contacted. Fourteen of the people who were originally sent questionnaires could not be contacted. 228 of the remaining 296 returned questionnaires, a response rate of 77%.

It is interesting to note that we discovered the same paradox in our sample of laity as Clark did in his study of members of Anglican church councils.[8] Although women attend church services in greater numbers than do men,[9] it seems that men are much more likely to be found in positions of responsibility. 61% of the lay members of the councils studied by Clark were men, and in our sample 72% were men.

Questionnaires were also sent to all Anglican clergy in the diocese. 213 out of 257 possible respondents returned their questionnaires, a response rate of 83%. Both questionnaires covered participation, influence, reform and ecumenism.

Lay Participation in Diocesan Affairs

In spite of the fact that our lay sample consists of members of the church who are constitutionally involved, our data indicate that lay activity in diocesan affairs is fairly minimal. Only 10% of our lay respondents held offices on deanery synods as distinct from being members, and 11%, as opposed to 34% of the clergy, were members of any of the diocesan committees. Consequently it was not surprising to find that 88% of the laity said that they never, or less than once a month, sent memos, written reports, notes and other correspondence to others in the diocese, and 75% said they never received such correspondence or received them less than once a month, as against figures of 39% and 9% respectively for the clergy. Similarly, 84% of the laity said that they never or hardly ever used the telephone on behalf of the diocese, as against 20% of the clergy.

What are the spheres of diocesan activity in which the laity see themselves either under employed or fairly well employed? We asked our lay respondents about their level of participation in a variety of areas. The two main areas where they seem to be fully employed are congregational social life and church bazaars and fetes in that over 70% of lay respondents reckoned that the laity do about the right amount. They seem to be active in three other spheres – wives and mothers, choir and services, and Sunday schools – with between 55% and 70% saying that the laity do about the right amount or too much. However, in the majority of the areas about which they were asked, our respondents claimed that the laity have little or nothing to do. In the following areas over 70% of the lay respondents maintained that the laity do nothing or else too little: visiting, case work, intercessions, co-operation with other parishes, confirmation instruction, house prayers, healing, industrial missions, spiritual counselling, attending services, Christian adult education, and theological discussions. In addition, between 60% and 70% said that the laity do nothing or too little with regard to social work in collaboration with other authorities, leadership of the community in social and political affairs, and drama. It would appear that the laity are involved in affairs of an essentially 'social' nature rather than religious and pastoral/social work matters.

There might be a temptation to argue that the laity want things this way, that they do not want to channel their energies into the church any more than they have to. We would argue that this is not the case. In response to a general question concerning the distribution of work in the diocese, 64% of the lay respondents affirmed the laity have too little work to do. Our data do not provide any answers to the obvious question as to why the laity do not do something about it. We feel, however, that the argument proffered by Thompson some years ago, as a result of his research on the members of the electoral roll in four Birmingham parishes, may well still have considerable substance.[10] He argued that because the role of the laity within the church has not been clearly articulated by the church itself, lay people are at a loss to discern what their functions are, although they felt that their role was very different from that of the clergy.

We also see here the operation of professional exclusiveness mentioned by Harrison.[11] Those who are involved on a day-to-day basis in the work of the church, i.e. clergy, are likely to fill the more important decision-making positions.

Lay Perceptions of the Distribution of Influence in the Diocese

The apparent fact that the laity are not as fully employed as they might like to be, along with the lack of a clear role definition, could be expected to affect the ways in which they view the distribution of influence in the diocese. When asked about the degree of centralization in the diocese, 81% of laity saw it as centralized. This compared with 63% of clergy.

We also asked our respondents about the relative influence of a number of office holders and bodies in the diocese. The minimum score is 1 for little or no influence through to 5 for very great influence, following the scheme of Tannenbaum.[12] Table 1 (below)

TABLE 1

Perceptions of Influence by Laity and Clergy
(mean scores)

	Laity (N=228) %	Clergy (N=213) %	Z	p
Bishop	4·13	4·02	−1·1677	N.S.
Suffragan Bishop	2·89	2·49	−4·0448	⟨0·001
Provost	2·29	1·57	−8·1392	⟨0·001
Archdeacons	3·20	3·08	−1·3624	N.S.
Rural Deans	2·29	1·99	−3·5861	⟨0·001
Incumbents	2·37	2·17	−1·8233	⟨0·05
Assistant Curates	1·43	1·40	−0·3800	N.S.
Diocesan Synod	2·70	2·70	−0·0693	N.S.
Deanery Synods	2·03	2·06	0·3844	N.S.
Laity	1·70	2·15	5·1581	⟨0·001

presents the mean scores for both samples. This table shows that the laity ascribe greater influence than the clergy to each position, except for the laity themselves. They see all positions and bodies as having more influence than themselves, other than the most lowly priest, the assistant curate; so that they rank themselves ninth out of ten, whereas the clergy rank the laity sixth. Moreover, the laity are not content with this state of affairs in that 79% believed that the laity exercise too little influence on diocesan affairs.

Our findings suggest that the laity see themselves as lying at the foot of a centralized hierarchy with minimal influence. These data, however, seem to be very different from those of Clark's study,[13] which showed that 79% of the members of church councils believed that the laity exercised sufficient control over church affairs, with only 19% saying that they exercise too little control. This apparent discrepancy may be explicable on the grounds that, by sampling council members Clark's respondents were providing answers concerning the parochial level, whereas our sample of members of deanery synods were explicitly being asked about their influence at diocesan level. The organizational level which is the referent may well be the crucial factor in explaining the seeming disparity between the two sets of findings.

The Laity and Church Reform

In this section we wish to examine the extent to which laity and clergy exhibit different degrees of proclivity towards reform. When presented with a general question concerning reform, the laity would appear to perceive less need for change than the clergy (93% of the clergy feel some kind of reform is needed, against 75% of laity, a statistically significant difference). There is a similar significant difference in attitudes towards reform of the Established nature of the Church of England, 49% of clergy desiring disestablishment or reform along the lines of the Church of Scotland, compared with 27% of laity.

Our investigation went much deeper than this in that we asked our respondents whether they were in favour of a wide variety of reforms in the church that have been discussed. Answers to general questions may be misleading and it is important to know which groups are in favour of specific reforms. One battery of reform items was derived from some of the proposals of two recent reports commissioned by the Church of England, the Paul and Morley Reports. Table 2 (p. 19) lists the proportions of the two samples in favour of each reform.

This table points to the importance of dealing with specific issues rather than eliciting overall statements concerning reform. Whereas the general questions on reform and the Establishment appear to suggest that the laity are more conservative than the clergy, this is only partially confirmed by the data in Table 2. On four of the items, namely the system of payment, a central register, substitution

TABLE 2

Clergy and Laity in Favour of some Recommendations of the Paul and Morley Reports

	Laity (N=228) %	Clergy (N=213) %	Z	p
A common stipendary fund for all the clergy	72·3	81·2	−2·1011	<0·02
One single system of payment of all clergy with increments for length of service and special responsibilities	86·4	85·0	0·4099	N.S.
Upon ordination, the placing of a man on the diocesan strength and payment of him, whether or not he has a job	58·3	70·4	−2·5640	<0·005
An open central register to bring available men in touch with available posts	97·2	93·2	−1·9260	<0·05
Substitution of Parson's leasehold for Parson's freehold (that is, a maximum of 15 years in any one parish)	59·9	59·3	0·1224	N.S.
The encouragement of groups and team ministries	78·0	80·7	−0·6749	N.S.
The establishment of lay street teams and other organized forms of lay activity in the parishes	80·5	95·7	−4·7962	<0·01
Stepping up of the co-ordinating work of rural deans and the status of rural deans	80·5	69·0	2·6842	<0·005

of leasehold, and group and team ministries, there is virtually no difference between the proportions of the two samples in favour of the recommendations. The clergy are more reform-oriented than the laity on three of the four remaining items, a stipendiary fund, established jobs and formal lay activity. The laity seem to be very concerned about the lack of effectiveness of the deanery level of the church and so endorse this item to a greater extent than do the clergy. Presumably their involvement with the synodical system at deanery level has brought about this difference. These findings suggest that we must treat with caution statements which tend to link conservatism and resistance to reform to one or another of these two groups within the church.

The Laity and Ecumenism

In this section we aim to examine the extent to which the two samples are in favour of a number of issues regarding the ecumeni-

TABLE 3

Laity and Clergy in Favour of Union with Specific Churches

	In favour		Against	
	n	%	n	%
Laity (N=228)				
Roman Catholic	131	(57·4)	97	(42·6)
Methodist	199	(87·2)	29	(12·8)
Baptist	154	(67·5)	74	(32·5)
Congregational	164	(71·9)	64	(28·1)
Presbyterian	146	(64·0)	82	(36·0)
Clergy (N=213)				
Roman Catholic	185	(86·8)	28	(13·2)
Methodist	197	(92·4)	26	(7·6)
Baptist	156	(73·2)	57	(26·8)
Congregational	166	(77·9)	47	(22·1)
Presbyterian	168	(78·8)	45	(21·2)
	X^2	p		
Roman Catholic	48·87	<0·001		
Methodist	4·09	<0·05		
Baptist	1·96	N.S.		
Congregational	2·43	N.S.		
Presbyterian	12·62	<0·001		

cal movement. Table 3 (p. 20) shows the numbers and percentages of both samples affirming that they were in favour of the eventual union of the Church of England with five major churches. The Congregational and Presbyterian Churches are treated separately because they had not united to form the United Reformed Church when these two surveys were carried out.

It can be seen that the laity were less in favour than the clergy of eventual union with each church. This difference in opinion was evident from the voting of the Church of England's General Synod in March 1972 on union with the Methodist Church which many people felt would be approved. When the House of Laity voted on union only 62·82% were in favour, this percentage being considerably lower than that of the House of Bishops and somewhat lower than that of the clergy. The data discussed here would indicate that the laity will constitute an even greater obstacle to unity with churches other than the Methodists, which is the church with which our sample of laity was most in favour of uniting.

The laity also seem to be much more resistant to organic union with the Roman Catholic Church than the clergy. Whereas Clark found that Anglican council members tended to be divided in their sympathy between the Methodist and the Roman Catholic Churches,[14] our data suggest that sympathy for the Roman Catholic Church *vis-à-vis* other denominations has declined somewhat. This could be explained on the grounds that many Anglicans might resent the apparent intransigence of Rome on matters like birth control and mixed marriages, over which the church has not budged since Clark's survey was carried out.

Anglican laity exhibit a different order of preferences for unity from Methodist laity, as suggested by the researches of Clark, Hill and Turner.[15] Methodist laity tend to favour the Congregational Church most of all with the Anglican, Baptist and Presbyterian churches being more or less equally favoured. Moreover, as Turner found, Methodist ministers in a Yorkshire district viewed church mergers more favourably than did the laity, which is comparable to our findings with regard to clergy-lay differences in desire for unity. However, whereas our research suggests that there is a sizeable proportion of laity in favour of organic union with all five churches, Turner was able to write: 'The major point of agreement between ministers and laity over ecumenism came with their mutual rejection of Roman Catholicism.'[16]

The apparent facts that Anglican laity and clergy differ in the extent and ranking of their preferences for union with other churches, and that Methodist laity seem to have a quite different set of preferences from those of Anglican laity, serves to point to the many basic problems that will have to be overcome before ecumenical negotiations fructify.

We also asked both our samples whether they were in favour of a variety of forms of ecumenical co-operation which stop short of unity. Table 4 (below) shows that clergy and laity are almost totally equal in their endorsement of these items.

TABLE 4

Laity and Clergy in Favour of some Forms of Ecumenical Co-operation

	Laity in favour (N=228) %	Clergy in favour (N=213) %
Clergy preaching in each other's churches	96·0	93·3
Jointly organized services with other churches	92·0	86·5
Joint meeting of clergy/ministers	96·5	98·1
Joint meetings of members	94·2	94·8
Joint study groups	92·9	94·3
Joint conferences	90·6	88·6
Joint publications*	79·2	88·5
Joint theological colleges	75·7	76·2
Joint education, social welfare and community projects	94·2	95·2
The sharing of churches	78·2	81·0

* significant at $<0·01$ level of confidence

These findings tend to differ from those of Glock, Ringer, and Babbie whose research indicated that parishioners in the Episcopalian Church – the nearest 'equivalent' in the United States to the Church of England – were more likely than clergy to favour services including Holy Communion and to accept a minister from a Protestant church preaching in the local church.[17] Our data suggest that clergy and laity are more or less equally strongly in favour of various forms of ecumenical co-operation, but that the laity are less in favour of organic union.

Conclusions

In spite of the fact that our sample of laity consisted of those lay people who are constitutionally involved in the work of the church, they appear to be only tangentially related to the work of the diocese. In addition, and related to this, they are in a relatively powerless position *vis-à-vis* most other people in the diocese. Our data tend to support the statement from a report to the Convocation of Canterbury in 1902 which noted that a 'primitive distinction' has always existed and will always exist between clergy and laity in spite of the fact that 'The study of the Apostolic and primitive constitution of the church, as it is set forth in Holy Scripture and in the history and writings of the first three centuries, shows . . . clearly the co-ordinate action of clergy and laity as integral parts of the whole body of Christ.'[18]

In spite of the introduction of synodical government, our findings suggest that, at least at diocesan level, this 'primitive distinction' will persist. The data would appear to support the view of one recent commentator on the introduction of synodical government:

> . . . in spite of these structural alterations it will be some time in most congregations before clerical domination is replaced by clerical-lay partnership . . . (Moreover) the clergy expect to dominate the church.[19]

This 'clerical domination' is underlined and reinforced by the fact that the laity rarely receive memos and various other forms of correspondence from others in the diocese, whereas clergy constantly complain about the weight of information they receive. Access to, and control of organizational information is a 'power resource' and the laity seem to be largely excluded from such access.[20] Clergy have the power that derives from their being full-time organizational officials involved in the networks of information and performing tasks which only they are allowed to fulfil. 'Clerical domination' is particularly evident in the ecumenical sphere with 52% of our sample of clergy belonging to an ecumenical group of one sort or another and only 18% of the laity belonging to one. This may be largely due to laity not joining such groups because they see ecumenical discussions as the prerogative of the religious specialist, especially since there may be some resentment of lay participation in such discussions. It is paradoxical perhaps that such a situation has arisen since, as Leslie Paul has pointed out,[21] the ecumenical movement began from within the ranks of the laity and not the clergy. Moreover, the virtual exclusion of the laity from influence and participation in the work of the church may well affect a whole range of attitudes and activities, of which ecumenical activity may only be an example.

To summarize, then, we find differences between clergy and laity in attitudes towards reform and organic union. With some reservations the laity are essentially more conservative, or alternatively, and perhaps more realistically, the clergy are more in line with the official policies of the church. This, we suggest, is in line with the organizational positions of the two groups, which is reflected in the differences between their perceptions of the influence structure of the diocese and the lack of participation in church affairs by the laity.

NOTES

1. The findings reported here are part of a wider study of the organization structure of churches financed by the Social Science Research Council, Grant No. HR/L020/1. For a statement of the aims of the overall study see C. Robin Hinings and Bruce D. Foster, 'The Organisation Structure of Churches', *Sociology*, vol. 7, no. 1, 1973, pp.93-106.

2. e.g. David B. Clark, *A Survey of Anglicans and Methodists in Four Towns*, Epworth Press 1965; Charles Y. Glock, Benjamin B. Ringer, and Earl R. Babbie, *To Comfort and to Challenge*, University of California Press 1967; Charles Y. Glock and Philip Roos, 'Parishioners' Views of how Ministers spend their Time', *Review of Religious Research*, vol. II, no. 4, 1961, pp.170-5; Paul M. Harrison, *Authority and Power in the Free Church Tradition*, Princeton University Press 1959; J. K. Hadden, *The Gathering Storm in the Churches*, Harper & Row, NY 1969; Steven E. Murphy, 'A note on Clergy-Laity differences among Lutherans', *Journal for the Scientific Study of Religion*, vol. 11, no. 2, 1972, pp.177-9.

3. Bryan Wilson, *Religion in Secular Society*, C. A. Watts 1966, p.165 (and Penguin Books 1969).

4. Barry Till, *The Churches Search for Unity*, Penguin Books 1972, pp.55, 57.

5. Harrison, op. cit., p.57.

6. S. M. Lipset, Martin Trow and James S. Coleman, *Union Democracy*, The Free Press of Glencoe 1956.

7. Andrew M. Pettigrew, 'Information Control as a Power Resource', *Sociology*, vol. 6, 1972, pp.187-204.

8. Clark, op. cit., p.19.

9. W. S. F. Pickering, 'The Present Position of the Anglican and Methodist Churches in the light of available Statistics', in *Anglican Methodist Relations*, ed. W. S. F. Pickering, Darton, Longman and Todd 1961, p.24.

10. R. H. T. Thompson, *The Church's Understanding of Itself*, SCM Press 1957, pp.93-5.

11. Harrison, op. cit.

12. Arnold S. Tannenbaum, *Control in Organisations*, McGraw-Hill, NY 1968.

13. Clark, op. cit., p.65.

14. Clark, op. cit., p.75.

15. Clark, op. cit.; Michael Hill and Peter Wakeford, 'Disembodied Ecumenicalism: a Survey of the Members of Four Methodist Churches in or near London', *A Sociological Yearbook of Religion in Britain 2*, ed. David Martin, SCM Press 1969, pp.19-46; Bryan Turner, 'Institutional Persistence and Ecumenicalism in Northern Methodism', *A Sociological Yearbook of Religion in Britain 2*, pp.47-57; Michael Hill and Bryan Turner, 'The Laity and Church Unity', *New Christian*, 17 April 1969, pp.6-7.

16. Turner, op. cit., p.54.

17. Glock, Ringer and Babbie, op. cit., pp.188-9.

18. Quoted in Leslie Paul, *The Deployment and Payment of the Clergy*, Church Information Office 1964, p.148.

19. Till, op. cit., pp.55, 57.

20. Pettigrew, op. cit.

21. Leslie Paul, *The Death and Resurrection of the Church*, Hodder & Stoughton 1968, p.115.

3 The Nature of Religion in Ireland

Malcolm Macourt

As a statistician, I am interested in the Census of Population. Recently I have turned my attention to the religious inquiry in the Irish Census. Apart from Horace Mann's Church Attendance Census in 1851, the English Census authorities have never got involved in the thorny problem of collecting data on religion. But a religious inquiry has been included in every major Census throughout Ireland starting in 1861 and continuing through to the recent 1971 Census.

No attempt is made here to discuss the efficiency of this form of inquiry in the collection of meaningful information about the religious acts or theological views of the Irish; rather, I am concerned to point to a confusion that has existed in and about Ireland – the confusion between religious organizations and tribal groupings.

Simply to place in a census schedule a column in which the respondent is asked to state his 'religious profession' poses questions about what is meant by 'religious profession'. While it might seem to an outsider a simple question (asked in rather archaic language), in Ireland it may be answered in two distinct but interlinked ways. It can be answered by giving the organizational label of the place of worship regularly attended (or with which the respondent is connected formally) – here communional or colloquially 'religious' – e.g. Reformed Presbyterian, Free Methodist; or it can be answered by giving the label of the social, cultural, political, national group with which the respondent identifies – here divisional or colloquially 'tribal' – e.g. Catholic, Protestant. The word 'communional' is chosen in favour of 'denominational' since the latter has a technical meaning imputed to it by Martin,[1] with which it might have been confused. The word 'divisional' is intended to reflect the divisions in society to which it points, and avoids the anthropological overtones contained in the word 'tribal'.

In this paper a typology of religious organizations is suggested which might help throw some light on the nature of the major communions. Consideration of this typology along with other typologies and with the nature of the system of social stratification helps clarify the difference between divisions and communions. The divisions are not sufficiently described as religious organizations but there is associated with each division a religious communion or communions. Several factors seem to be involved in the divisional classification, of which only one is religion; others include culture, politics and nationality.

The tables in the Appendix provide a short synopsis of the summary data published.

A Typology of Religious Organizations

It will be shown that, when considered as religious organizations, the Roman Catholic Church, the Church of Ireland, and the Presbyterian Church in Ireland in the nineteenth century were what will be labelled 'quasi-churches', and that the same label can be given to the Roman Catholic Church today. Similarly semi-establishment Protestantism in Northern Ireland can be considered in a like manner, even though it does not exist as a formal body, as can the religious 'minority' (if considered as a conglomerate religious body) in the Republic. Other religious organizations can be considered either as 'internal splinter-groups' or as 'minority religious groups'.

A 'quasi-church' can be regarded as a 'church', except that it fails to achieve, or does not attempt to achieve, universality because of geographical, class or cultural boundaries. By a 'church' is meant a universal religious organization which is the repository of all the values and mores of society, which largely accepts the social order of society, and which has birthright membership. Here use is made of Troeltsch's notion of a 'church',[2] and of Becker's notion of an 'ecclesia'.[3]

An 'internal splinter-group' is a separate religious communion which shares many of its basic beliefs or its form of church organization with, and because of a disagreement has emerged from, one of the 'quasi-churches'. No example of an 'internal splinter-group' from the Roman Catholic Church is apparent in Ireland, but there are several examples from both the Church of Ireland, and from the Presbyterian Church.

The phrase 'minority religious groups' is meant to denote an all-embracing 'others' category, which of course includes 'sects' – exclusive groups with their own means of salvation[4] – as well as other small religious communions. They have always accounted for less than 1% of the total population of the island.

The Roman Catholic Church

The dominant position of the Roman Catholic Church throughout the entire island, and particularly in the Republic, would suggest that it could be described as a 'quasi-church' in that it can be seen over the whole period as claiming to be the universal religious organization for the Irish people. The Church has certainly dominated the masses, and upheld the order of society, although it was not until the setting up of the Irish Free State that it could be said fully to accept the structure of the state. Since the Treaty it has identified itself closely with the state, persuading the political authority to accept its (the Church's) authority in matters of morals and education. The Roman Catholic Church regards itself as comprising all the Irish people, save for an 'odd' minority. The Irish Hierarchy have shown themselves slow to accept some of the official statements of the Church after the Second Vatican Council concerning relationships with and attitudes towards members of other Christian communions, giving the impression to some that they are loth to allow any shift in their stated position as the Church of the Irish people.[5]

In Northern Ireland, although there are large areas in which the Roman Catholic Church claims the allegiance of the majority of the inhabitants, in few of these areas is it in an overwhelming majority and for most of the centres of population it is in a minority. Nonetheless, the Roman Catholic Church claims jurisdiction over a certain section of the people, a limited universe, and in the main, it does not seek to evangelize beyond those who 'belong' to it. It regards these 'belongers' as within its jurisdiction whether or not they actually have any active connection with its beliefs and practices, and it recognizes that it has no claim over other people.[6] Further, in the Republic the attitude of the Roman

Catholic Church towards the 'minority' now, one of polite toleration or one of mild acceptance, bears out this notion of limited universality, although of course the limitation is only to the extent of 5% of the population.

The Church of Ireland

The Church of Ireland has had three distinct phases since the first religious Census in 1861. As part of the United Church of England and Ireland it was the Established Church of the island until the coming into force, on 1 January 1871, of the Irish Church Act, 1869. From then until the Treaty recognizing the Irish Free State it was the largest minority church in the island, and the church of a disproportionately large number of those administering the island, whether as civil servants, local government officials or military officers.[7] Within this period it had a position of superiority in the professions, in land ownership, and in business and commerce throughout the island far in excess of that justified by its numerical strength.[8] After the Treaty, the Church of Ireland became one of three major, and approximately equal groups in the North, and in the Republic it became the second church, although it commanded the allegiance of less than 6% of the population in 1926.

First phase – establishment

In the first phase the Church of Ireland can readily be typified throughout the island as a 'quasi-church'. Its position as the 'legal establishment' placed it on a par with the established churches in other parts of the British Isles, although it differed from each of the others.

The Church of England, despite (or perhaps because of) the results of the collateral Census inquiry into church attendance in 1851, could regard itself as being the church of the majority of the English population.[9] The Church of Scotland, after the disruption of 1843 and the formation of the United Presbyterian Church in 1847, was faced with two major alternative non-established Presbyterian bodies, who together prevented it from claiming to be the church of the majority of the population of Scotland; although even then it could claim to share a basic theological position with both the United Presbyterian Church and the

Free Church. Thus the Established Church could claim that a large majority of the people were associated with Presbyterian bodies who were in basic agreement on theological matters and differed only on administrative questions, particularly their attitude towards 'establishment'.

The Established Church in Wales, the Church in Wales, could still claim in 1910 the allegiance of a much higher percentage of the people of Wales, than could the Church of Ireland claim at any time since the start of data collection. In the Report of the Royal Commission on the Church of England and other religious bodies in Wales and Monmouthshire in 1910, which preceded the disestablishment of the church, the numbers given of communicants (or fully admitted members in the cases of religious communions other than the Established Church) showed the Established Church to be in the minority, but also showed it to be the largest communion in Wales.

The established churches in England and Scotland could at least be said to exhibit the characteristics of 'churches', rather than those of 'quasi-churches', while on the other hand the established churches in Wales and Ireland were 'quasi-churches' rather than 'churches'.

Second phase – social dominance

The limitation on the universality of the Church of Ireland's position is best seen in the second phase, when the disestablished church adopted its own position on theological matters and questions of church order. The separation from the Church of England, and the disestablishment, took place at a time when the Tractarian party in the Church of England was very powerful. Partly as a reaction to this party, partly as a reaction to the ritualism of Roman Catholicism in Ireland, and partly in an attempt to be seen as a body separate from the Church of England, entitled to respect as an Irish institution, the new body adopted a 'low' church stance on matters of church order, and emphasized its claim to be the original Catholic Celtic Church.[10] Notwithstanding its attempts at individuality, and particularly its attempts to prove itself authentically Irish, the Church of Ireland was generally regarded as the Church of the English, of the Anglo-Irish, and of those planters in Ulster who originated in England.[11]

Third phase – part of a 'quasi-church'

In the period since the Treaty it is important to consider the two parts of the island separately. In Northern Ireland, the third phase has seen the Church of Ireland show distinct signs of transforming itself into a section within Protestantism. The Church of Ireland has become, along with the Presbyterian Church and the Methodist Church, one of the sections of semi-established Protestantism. Little attempt is made to convince members or nonmembers that the church has a unique message, and it no longer tries to identify, neither is it so identified by others, with the 'English' elements in society; it can be seen as a parallel to the Presbyterian Church in size and in its theological doctrines and its common acceptance of the basis of the social order of society in the province. However the process is not complete as the requirement on its clergy, imposed by the church and not by the State, that they must provide the rites of the church (baptism and burial particularly) for all for whom they are requested, suggests that there is some residual vestige of universal birthright membership.[12] The talks at present taking place between the three major Protestant communions in Ireland, in so far as they are now concentrating on organizational matters, after having quickly reached broad agreement on theological questions,[13] can be seen as an acceptance of a common position as parts of a larger 'quasi-church'.

The position of the Church of Ireland in the Republic of Ireland is slightly different. Being by far the largest of the minority religious communions its leaders are generally regarded as the leaders of the religious minority (even to the extent of token 'minority' representation at state occasions being provided by the Church of Ireland), and it is popularly referred to as the Protestant Church – although there may be historical reasons for this label. On the disestablishment the Church was named 'the Protestant Episcopal Church of Ireland' by the State, and it was only after a legal ruling that the shorter title 'Church of Ireland' was recognized. The title 'Protestant', although coined earlier, may have received some reinforcement from this period. Remembering that the representatives to the inter-church talks from all three bodies concerned come from both parts of the island, here again we can consider the situation as that of a Protestant body which can be labelled a 'quasi-church', the body comprising the Church of Ireland as its major element, with the Presbyterian Church and the Methodist Church also involved.

The Presbyterian Church in Ireland

There are many bodies in Ireland which include the word 'presbyterian' in their title. Most of these were formed as the result of disputes over theology or church organization within the orthodox body, now the Presbyterian Church in Ireland; this body comprises those Presbyteries which are constituent parts of the General Assembly of the Presbyterian Church in Ireland. The other bodies, e.g. Reformed Presbyterians (from 1690 in Scotland, 1796 in Ireland), Non-Subscribing Presbyterians (from 1726 and 1830)[14] and Evangelical Presbyterians (from 1927), can be seen as 'internal splinter-groups'.

The Presbyterian Church has never been island wide, although it does have constituent congregations in most of the 32 counties. Excluding the historic province of Ulster and the City and County of Dublin, the Presbyterians have never accounted for more than 0·5% of the population, and in 1961 accounted for only 0·13% of the population. However, in Ulster, and elsewhere it could be maintained that the Presbyterian body in the nineteenth century was the Scots Church (a title which certain individual churches hold until the present), and the church regarded itself as 'the eldest daughter of the Scottish Kirk'.[15] It was primarily the church of those planters and settlers who originated in Scotland. The body was certainly formed by these settlers, and following the failure of the Episcopal Church to come to an accommodation with its leaders in the seventeenth and eighteenth centuries, it continued to be supported almost exclusively by the descendants of these settlers. The existence of disabilities in the eighteenth century concerning the holding of public office caused the Presbyterians, as a body, to be set over against the order of the State, although they may be seen as preserving the values of their own sub-state (of settlers in a heathen land).

Since the Treaty the position of the Presbyterian Church in Northern Ireland has been that of the larger of two major Protestant Churches, wielding much power, and being at one with the State in general principle. As with the Church of Ireland, it can be seen as part of a larger 'quasi-church'. In the Republic outside the border counties, the 7,000 Presbyterians (of whom 5,000 live in the Dublin area) are a small subsection of Protestantism, as are the Methodists (5,500, of whom 3,000 live in the Dublin area). These two communions share many characteristics with the Church of Ireland such as high occupational status predomination and low fertility.[16]

Other Religious Communions

As has already been suggested the position of the Methodist Church both in Northern Ireland and in the Republic since the Treaty is that of part of a large 'quasi-church'. We find several references in the data sources to changes in the status and organization of the Methodists before the Treaty. The Members of the Royal Commission on Public Instruction of 1834, who conducted a sort of religious Census, noted in their report that there were included in the number of members reported for the Established Church a considerable number of Wesleyan Methodists 'who, although attending religious service in other places of worship, consider themselves to be in connection with the Established Church and wished to be classed as members of that body'.[17] By the time of the 1861 Census (the first to include the religious inquiry), we find that it was noted by a correspondent, 'A Northern Clergyman', to one of the Dublin newspapers, the *Irish Times* (3 April 1861) that the Wesleyans had a separate communion but that the Primitive Methodists were still part of the Established Church. Something more of this segmentation of Methodism, between those formally separating themselves from the Church of Ireland and those remaining technically within it, is found in the memorandum[18] sent by the Secretary of the Census Commissioners to enumerators in 1891 for their guidance when entering details of religious professions in summary tables which they were required to prepare. Primitive Church Methodists were to be categorized as 'Protestant Episcopalian' (the Commissioners' name for the Church of Ireland), whereas Primitive Methodists *inter alia* were to be categorized as Methodists. This evidence suggests that in the period before the Treaty the various sections of Methodism may be regarded as 'internal splinter-groups' from the Church of Ireland.

A similar case could be made out for the Brethren, as an 'internal splinter-group' from the Church of Ireland.[19] Many other smaller religious communions exist in Ireland; these, with the exceptions noted, are here labelled 'minority religious groups'.

Communion or Division

The typology presented yields three 'quasi-churches' in the nineteenth century, and two in the present day. Apart from the Roman Catholic Church, 'internal splinter-groups' can be identified for these 'quasi-churches'. These small religious groups retain much in common with their associated 'quasi-church'.

Particularly in the nineteenth century, but also up to the present, it would appear that to state one's religious profession as Presbyterian, with or without a preceding adjective, was not necessarily to make any personal profession about the status of the Westminster Confession of Faith, or to give assent to the presbyterial form of church government, or even (for an adult) to state that one was in membership with any congregation claiming to be Presbyterian. Rather it was to assert something about a way of life, about one's family heritage. This heritage included general acceptance, as part of its fabric, of Presbyterian congregations, but it was more than, and sometimes other than, theological statements, or assertions about the best form of church government.[20] Similiar comments could be made of those who state their profession as Church of Ireland or as Roman Catholic.

Each of these 'quasi-churches', then, can be seen as providing the religious and theological dimension in a multi-dimensional division of Irish society. These divisions contain political, cultural and social dimensions as well as the religious one, although the names by which they are best known reflect the religious dimension primarily. The divisions which exist in Irish society are: Protestant and Catholic in this century; Protestant, Presbyterian and Catholic in the last. In the last century 'Protestant' was used as a religious label to refer to members of the Established Church, Protestant as a divisional label referred to those within the ambit of the establishment. Presbyterian referred to those, predominantly living in the historic province of Ulster and not Roman Catholics, who claimed Scots ancestry and whose society, both agricultural and industrial, cherished its individuality and its separate customs. In Northern Ireland. 'Protestant' now refers to those who seek to continue this northern dissenting culture, with its ties with Great Britain, but with its desire to maintain its distinctive heritage; it is a group which contains, among others, members of the Church of Ireland and Methodists as well as Presbyterians. In the Republic, the divisions which now have less political content but more social and cultural content are Catholic and 'the rest', politely known as 'the minority'.

When considering the 'quasi-churches' as religious organizations they are collectively labelled 'communions', and the classification as 'communional'; but when we are considering the multi-dimensional entities they are collectively labelled 'divisions', and the classification as 'divisional'. In this context the 'internal splinter-groups' and the 'minority religious groups' are also labelled communions.

System of Social Stratification

We can gain some insight into these divisions, and into the society of which they are a part, if we consider the sort of social stratification involved. Four separate notions appear to be important in any attempt to describe Irish social stratification and the relationship of divisions within it and to it. They are: the singularity of ethnic unit; the mode of recruitment to any group; the cultural distinction of the groups; and the existence of a ranking of groups within society.

Ethnic unit

It is difficult to accept fully either that Ireland's people are one ethnic unit, or that the three separate groups are themselves ethnic units. The major influx of planters and settlers into Ulster took place as long ago as the first half of the seventeenth century. There has been some intermarriage between the groups and there is no obvious difference between the groups (e.g. colour, language). However the attitude is still found in parts of 'Ulsterdom' that the settlers were sent by God to the heathen land, and there is the parallel view that the Protestants are merely the tools of colonization of the British Empire. It is not unusual to find Protestants both in the Republic and in Northern Ireland referring to themselves as a tribe,[21] and while they may not be using the word in an accepted anthropological sense they are nonetheless emphasizing their difference from the Catholic population by their use of this label.

Dr Robert Moore in a recent paper in the journal *Race*[22] has attempted to show that the Northern Ireland situation is best typified in an imperial/colonial model, and suggests that reference to race-relations considerations may be more meaningful than any other. The imperial/colonial model may be appropriate for consideration of the Republic before the Treaty, but the majority position of the Protestants in Northern Ireland, and their belief that it is their country, albeit with links with Great Britain, suggest that the model is inapplicable to present-day Northern Ireland. Similarly, the continued existence of a small 'minority' community in the Republic, who no longer have emotional ties with Great Britain, suggests that the analysis is no longer applicable there.

Mode of recruitment

The major problem encountered in interpreting data from the Census arises from considerations of mode of recruitment to groups. An ardent Northern republican might find himself, without any change of political perspective, doubting papal infallibility or transubstantiation, and he might consequently transfer his allegiance to 'high' Anglicanism, thus finding himself recategorized as a Protestant, with all its political and cultural overtones. Or an avowed Presbyterian might decide (as did, among others, Rev. W. S. Armour, an eminent northern Presbyterian minister who became involved in the Home Rule debate) that some form of united independent Ireland was to be preferred to the existing political system, without ever contemplating any change in theological position. In the recent strife, I have been aware that several mixed marriage partners have been threatened by extremists from the 'side' to which both partners to the marriage are now religiously committed, since apparently both partners are suspected of association with the 'other side'.

Professor J. M. Barkley, the leading Presbyterian church historian, has remarked in a contribution to a recent pamphlet:

If a member of the Church of Ireland [or a Presbyterian] became a [Roman] Catholic or 'turned', to use the common term, he was never regarded as having done so on theological or philosophical grounds. He had let the side down. He might be ostracized and cut off. He might even be subject to physical attack by locals. He had betrayed the tribe.[23]

Membership of a division is normally, then, by ascription at birth, but a change in division, while not necessarily fully acceptable as a complete change, may be acquired.

Cultural distinction

The cultural distinction between the communities in Northern Ireland has been well documented.[24] Suffice it to say here that there is felt to be a cultural divide between the two communities in Northern Ireland. Even the use of the word 'communities' in normal reportage is an indicator of this. It is not, however, accepted that there are no links across this divide, nor is it accepted that the situation is static. Particularly in middle-class society, we find the emergence of a single class-based culture that combines parts of the traditions of 'Ulsterdom' with those of Ireland, and adds to them an acquired set of English values and interests. The political pronouncements of the newly-formed Alliance Party,[25] which has had considerable electoral success in middle-class areas, show this emerging cross-cultural unity very well.

In the Republic, however, the old divide between on the one hand a Protestant culture dominated by the 'West Britons'[26] – those of English birth or descent who constantly looked over their shoulders to what was happening 'back home', exemplified by many of the Irish Government civil servants before the Treaty and the smaller Anglo-Irish landlords who spent much of their time on their land before the passing of the Land Acts – and on the other hand the peasant Irish, has gone. It has developed through a cultural elitism on the part of the remaining Protestants, a benevolent paternalism, which could (if one looks at the Southern States of the USA) be likened to the best in the landowner attitude towards the Negro, to being the core of upper middle-class rural and urban society. The Protestants of Dublin, while forming no more than 25% of the senior administrative and professional personnel,[27] perhaps because they are without the inhibiting force of a conservative and isolationist hierarchy, have maintained a position of domination of upper middle-class culture and have been involved in the vanguard of developments in that culture, despite the declining numbers involved. In the rural areas it is emphasis on theological position that keeps the cultural divide in place between the large Protestant farmers and their Roman Catholic counterparts. The absence of a sizeable Protestant urban working class,[28] and the almost total non-existence of a Protestant agricultural working class[29] (outside the border areas), maintain the cultural divide between Protestants and working-class Roman Catholics.

Both in Northern Ireland, then, and in the Republic of Ireland, we find that there is cultural distinctiveness, but it is becoming difficult to distinguish it from the cultural continuum expected in a class-ordered society.

The ranking of groups

The ranking of the groups discussed could be said to have been established by law, in that 'legal' Protestants have been involved in government through the last two hundred years (since the establishment of the first modern 'democratic' parliament in Ireland in 1782). Presbyterians have had certain restrictions placed upon them from time to time, whereas for a long time there were many restrictions on the part that Roman Catholics could play in government, and in the leadership of society. This ordering (Protestant/ Presbyterian/Roman Catholic) remained until the Treaty, when the first two in combination took over supremacy of the Northern State, forcing Roman Catholics into a second class position.[30] The recent history of the Republic suggests that the minority are ranked higher than Catholics in every field of activity save politics.[31]

In considering how the divisions relate to the system of social stratification in Ireland it is necessary to look for the existence of restrictions limiting interaction between the divisions. Insistence on separate educational facilities operated by the minority in the Republic and by the Roman Catholics in Northern Ireland can be seen as restrictions on interaction. Publicly, the reasons given for this insistence are different. It is for theological reasons – to teach the faith – in the North, but in the Republic it is to avoid being swamped in what is regarded as a monocultural society. Further the practices adopted by the bishops of the Roman Catholic Church, whether in strict accord with the provisions of (successively) the Tametsi decree and the Ne Temere decree or not, have vested in them effective instruments of social control over intermarriage, and in this respect the liberalizing of the attitude of the Roman Catholic Church internationally appears to have been slow to reach Ireland.[32]

The recent strife in Northern Ireland can be seen as an attempt, on the part of some, to break-up the solidification of a division-orientated system of social stratification. The claim for 'civil rights' by Roman Catholics (supported by liberal Protestants initially) can be seen as an attempt, by a socially inferior status group, to emulate their superiors. Alternatively the oft-repeated claim that standards in Northern Ireland should be the same as those in Great Britain (legal sanctions against discrimination, change in the franchise, etc.) can be seen as the urging of the adoption of a reference group wherein the society's traditional status considerations are irrelevant and can be seen as analogous to the reported[33] move towards westernization urged by members of inferior castes in India.

Conclusion

It should really be obvious that to try to understand the divisions of Irish society only by considering the religious and organizational aspects of religious organizations, is to lose important social, cultural and political dimensions in the divisions. In considering the nature of the variable which might be measured by a 'religious profession' inquiry in the Census of Ireland we must be aware that two sorts of classification exist and are liable to be confused. There are communions – religious and theological organizations – and divisions – where political, cultural, social and national factors are uppermost.

Data Appendix

Census data show us that only three groups in Ireland have ever been able to command the allegiance of more than 2% of the population of the entire island at any census in which an inquiry into religious profession has been included. These are the Roman Catholic Church, the Church of Ireland, and the Presbyterian Church in Ireland. At each census these three have accounted, between them, for at least 95% of the population of the island. Roman Catholics have accounted for between 73·9% and 77·7% of the population, Church of Ireland for between 10·5% and 13·2% and Presbyterians for between 9·0% and 10·2%. Of the remainder, by far the largest group has been, and remains, the Methodist Church, accounting for between 0·8% and 1·9% of the population, that is for between 40% and 60% of the residual [See Table 1].

If we look at the two political divisions of the island, we find that in Northern Ireland each of these three major groups has always accounted for at least 20% of the population, whereas the fourth group, the Methodists, has never accounted for more than 5·1%. Together the three major groups have accounted for between 88·1% and 96·6% of the population, with no one group ever exceeding 41% of the total [See Table 2]. In the Republic of Ireland, Roman Catholics have always accounted for at least 89·4%, and in 1961 they accounted for 94·9% of the total. Of those remaining, the Church of Ireland has accounted for between 71·8% and 79·5%, the Presbyterians for between 13·1% and 14·7%, the Methodists for between 3·6% and 5·1%; between them these three groups have accounted for between 89·4% and 97·4% of the non-Roman Catholic population [See Table 3].

TABLE 1

Ireland

Year	Total	Roman Catholic	Church of Ireland	Presby-terian	Methodist	Others
1861[ab]	5,796,685	4,505,265 77·72%	693,357 11·96%	523,291 9·03%	45,399 0·78%	29,373 0·51%
1911[e]	4,390,219	3,242,670 73·86%	576,611 13·13%	440,525 10·04%	62,382 1·42%	68,031 1·55%
1926[f]	4,228,553	3,171,697 75·01%	502,939 11·89%	425,803 10·07%	60,217 1·42%	67,897 1·61%
1961[f]	4,243,383	3,171,020 74·73%	448,816 10·58%	432,066 10·18%	78,541 1·85%	112,940 2·66%

TABLE 2

Northern Ireland

Year	Total	Roman Catholic	Church of Ireland	Presbyterian	Methodist	Others
1861ac	1,396,183	571,690 40·95%	320,725 22·97%	457,119 32·74%	27,919 2·00%	18,730 1·34%
1911e	1,250,531	430,161 34·40%	327,076 26·16%	395,039 31·59%	45,942 3·67%	52,313 4·18%
1926g	1,256,561	420,428 33·46%	338,724 26·96%	393,374 31·30%	49,554 3·94%	54,481 4·34%
1961j	1,425,042	497,547 34·91%	344,800 24·20%	413,113 28·99%	71,865 5·04%	97,717 6·86%

TABLE 3

Republic of Ireland

Year	Total	Roman Catholic	Church of Ireland	Presbyterian	Methodist	Others
1861ad	4,400,502	3,933,575 89·39%	372,632 8·47%	66,172 1·50%	17,480 0·40%	10,643 0·24%
1911d	3,139,688	2,812,509 89·58%	249,535 7·95%	45,486 1·45%	16,440 0·52%	15,718 0·50%
1926h	2,971,992	2,751,269 92·57%	164,215 5·53%	32,429 1·09%	10,663 0·36%	13,416 0·45%
1961k	2,818,341	2,673,473 94·86%	104,016 3·69%	18,953 0·67%	6,676 0·24%	15,223 0·54%

a Excluding Merchant Seamen and others who were enumerated in Ireland on English Census forms only.
b Census of Population, Ireland, 1861, Report on Religions and Education, Parliamentary Papers 1863, *60*, pp. 558 and 560.
c Ibid., pp. 408, 420, 466, 557-8.
d By subtraction.
e Census of Population, Ireland, 1911, General Report, Parliamentary Papers 1912-13, *118*, p. 211.
f By addition.
g Census of Population, Northern Ireland, 1961, Preliminary Report, pp. 28, 29.
h Census of Population, Saorstat Eireann, 1926, vol. III (I), p. 3.
j Census of Population of Ireland, 1961, vol. VII (I), p. 1.
k Compiled from Census of Population, 1961, Northern Ireland, County Reports, Table 18 in each volume.

NOTES

1. David A. Martin, 'The Denomination', *British Journal of Sociology*, 13, 1962, pp.1-14.
2. Ernst Troeltsch, *The Social Teaching of the Christian Churches*, Allen & Unwin 1931.
3. Howard Becker, *Systematic Sociology ... of Leopold von Wiese*, John Wiley, NY 1932.
4. As in for example Roland Robertson, *The Sociological Interpretation of Religion*, Blackwell 1970, pp.120-38.
5. For a full discussion of the relationships between the Roman Catholic Church and the State in the Republic of Ireland see J. H. Whyte, *Church and State in Modern Ireland, 1923-70*, Gill & Macmillan 1971.
6. Here there is some similarity with Mehl's concept of a 'minority church' as used in the Canadian study of Millett. See David Millett, 'A Typology of Religious Organisations suggested by the Canadian Census', *Sociology Analysis*, 30 (2), 1969, pp.112-13.
7. Army Officers: Church of Ireland (C of I) 1783, Roman Catholic (RC) 304, others 121; Soldiers and Non-Commissioned Officers: C of I 16,570, RC 6,440, others 3,242; Local Government Officers: C of I 1,063, RC 2,629, others 565; Civil Service Officers and Clerks: C of I 1,926, RC 4,140, others 951. General Report of the Census of Ireland, 1911, p.p. 1912-13 *118*, p.9. The predominance of the Church of Ireland is even more striking if one considers high ranking officials. Hamilton, in his *History of the Irish Presbyterian Church* quotes data from Rev. J. W. Whigham, *Presbyterian Map of Ireland*, 1886 (place and publisher not given) from which it can be calculated that of those of the rank of District Inspector or above in the Constabulary: C of I 222, RC 47, Pres. 5; and of those senior government servants in several posts listed: C of I 75, RC 48, Pres. 17. See Rev. Thomas Hamilton, *History of the Irish Presbyterian Church*, T. & T. Clark (Special Edition) 1887, p.191.
8. Barristers and Solicitors: C of I 845, RC 999, others 402; Physicians, Surgeons and General Practitioners: C of I 649, RC 1,084, others 493; Brokers, Agents and Factors: C of I 861, RC 1,277, others 815; Auctioneers, Appraisers, Valuers and House Agents: C of I 413, RC 426, others 240; Bankers and those in Bank Service: C of I 1,267, RC 1,080, others 686. General Report of the Census of Ireland, 1911, pp.9-10. Hamilton quotes data from Whigham showing that of Judges (whether County Court or otherwise) and Resident Magistrates: C of I 78, RC 36, Pres. 5. Hamilton, *History of the Irish Presbyterian Church*, p.191.
9. See the calculations of Mann in Horace Mann, 'On the Statistical Position of Religious Bodies in England and Wales', *Journal of Statistical Society of London*, 18, 1855, pp.150-3.
10. See Gabriel Daly, 'Church Renewal: 1869-1877' in *Irish Anglicanism 1869-1969*, ed. Michael Hurley, Allen Figgis, Dublin 1970, pp.23-38.
11. This point is made by many historians. Perhaps the most readable general histories are J. C. Beckett, *A Short History of Ireland*, Hutchinson 1958 (revised edition) and F. S. L. Lyons, *Ireland Since the Famine*, Weidenfeld & Nicholson 1971. Also relevant is Donald Harman Akenson, *The Church of Ireland – Ecclesiastical Reform and Revolution, 1800-1885*, Yale University Press 1971.

12. Canon 33 of the Church of Ireland states that

No minister ... shall refuse ... to christen ... any child that is brought to the Church to him ... to be christened, either of whose parents are resident within his cure; or to bury ... any person who may have died within his cure.

The Constitution of the Church of Ireland, ed. J. L. B. Deane, APCK, Dublin 1972 (revised edition), p.154.

13. See the report for 1972-3 'Towards a United Church – Tripartite Conversations' presented to the ruling bodies of the three churches at their annual meetings in 1973, e.g. 'General Synod of the Church of Ireland, 1973, Reports', pp.187-215.

14. There are good general discussions of the divisions within Presbyterianism in William Thomas Latimer, *A History of the Irish Presbyterians*, Cleeland and Mullan & Son, Belfast 1902, and James B. Woodburn, *The Ulster Scot*, Allenson, London 1914.

15. This is a phrase often used in church pronouncements. It probably originates from the sentiments expressed in the Act of Union between the Synod of Ulster and the Associate Synod (the Seceders) forming the General Assembly of the Presbyterian Church in Ireland

holding the standards and adopting the Discipline of the parent Church of Scotland ... these two churches do unite under the same standards as aforesaid.

Minutes of the General Assembly ..., 1840, pp.3-4.

16. See Brendan M. Walsh, *Religion and Demographic Behaviour in Ireland*, Economic and Social Research Institute, Paper No. 55, Dublin 1970.

17. First Report of the Commissioners of Public Instruction, Ireland, p.p. 1835, *33*, p.5.

18. General Report of the Census of Ireland, 1891, p.p. 1892, *90*, Appendix, p.544.

19. For example we find in a leading article in 1881 on the Census, the editor of the *Irish Ecclesiastical Gazette*, the major Church of Ireland journal of the period, stating

We have much reason to apprehend that the next Census will prove only too truly, the accuracy of what was stated so often by the Lord Primate and others in the General Synod, that we have lost not a few to Plymouth Brethrenism ... we may fairly place their gain to our loss.

Irish Ecclesiastical Gazette, 23, 19.3.1881, p.192.

20. See particularly Woodburn, *The Ulster Scot*, pp.382-401.

21. See, for example, the quotation from Professor J. M. Barkley, p.36 (and note 23) and private communication from an eminent Dublin journalist, who is a Protestant, Jack White. I understand from him that White uses the notion of a tribe extensively in his forthcoming book on the Protestant Minority in the Republic of Ireland.

22. Robert Moore, 'Race Relations in the Six Counties: Colonialism, Industrialization, and Stratification in Ireland', *RACE, 14* (1), July 1972, pp.21-42.

23. *Tribalism or Christianity in Ireland?*, New Ulster Movement, Belfast, September 1973. The quotation is from Part I – Christianity in Ireland.

24. See for example Conor Cruise O'Brien, *States of Ireland*, Hutchinson 1972; Denis P. Barritt and Charles F. Carter, *The Northern Ireland Problem*,

OUP 1962; and Rosemary Harris, *Prejudice and Tolerance in Ulster: A Study of Neighbours and 'Strangers' in a Border Community*, Manchester University Press 1972.

25. See particularly their election propaganda for the 1973 District and Constituent Assembly elections.

26. See Brian Inglis, *West Briton*, Faber 1962, and Viney's comments on it, published in the *Irish Times* of 26 March 1965 and reprinted as a pamphlet along with other articles in Michael Viney, *The Five Per Cent – A survey of Protestants in the Republic*, *Irish Times*, Dublin 1965.

27. For 1961 in the Republic as a whole, 26·3% of 'Directors, Managers and Company Secretaries' were not Roman Catholic. Census of Population of Ireland, 1961, vol. VII (I), table 11, pp.75, 76.

Taking the two socio-economic groups 'Higher Professional' and 'Employers and Managers' together, 16·5% were not Roman Catholic. This is clear from data given to me by the Census of Population Division, Central Statistics Office, Dublin, compared with Census of Population of Ireland, 1961, vol. III, table 7, p.120. Those not Roman Catholics formed 25% of 'Professionally qualified and high administrative' and 19% of 'Managerial and executive' respondents in Hutchinson's survey of Dublin. See Bertram Hutchinson, *Social Status and Inter-generational Social Mobility in Dublin*, Economic and Social Research Institute, Paper No. 48, Dublin 1969, p.6.

28. Hutchinson (art. cit., p.6) found that for Dublin only, only 25·4% of those respondents who were not Roman Catholic were in the groups 'skilled manual and routine grades of non-manual', 'semi-skilled manual' and 'unskilled manual', as against 66·1% of Roman Catholic respondents. For the Republic as a whole, Census data for 1961 shows that of those in non-agricultural occupations those in social groups 'other non-manual', 'skilled manual', 'semi-skilled manual' and 'unskilled manual' were 66·7% of Roman Catholics and 35·7% of non-Roman Catholics. Census of Population of Ireland, 1961, vol. III, table 7, p.120, compared with data given me by the Census of Population Division, Census of Population, Dublin.

29. Of 59,557 agricultural labourers, 1,018 were Church of Ireland, and 365 Presbyterian. Census of Population of Ireland, 1961, vol VII (I), table 11, pp.75, 76. The large number of Presbyterians in relation to the number of Church of Ireland would suggest that a disproportionately large number of both groups are in counties Cavan, Monaghan and Donegal, where the proportion of Presbyterians is highest. See also comments in my paper, 'An exploratory comparative study of Protestant and Catholic farmers in Ireland', *Economic and Social Review*, 4 (4), 1973, pp.511-22, particularly p.515.

30. For a reasoned statement of this case see *The Future of Northern Ireland – a Paper for Discussion*, Northern Ireland Office, HMSO 1972 – the 'green' paper.

31. See J. H. Whyte, 'Political Life in the South' in *Irish Anglicanism, 1869-1969*, ed. Hurley, pp.143-53.

32. See Raymond M. Lee, 'Putting *Ne Temere* in Context: Mixed Marriages and Canon Law in Ireland Before and After 1908', unpublished paper made available by the author, being a development of his paper 'Mixed Marriages and the Canon Law: The Irish Case' given at the Conference on the Conflict in Northern Ireland, Social and Political Aspects, Lancaster University, December 1971.

33. For example see Gerald D. Berreman, 'Caste' in *International Encyclopaedia of the Social Sciences,* ed. David Sills, vol. 2, Macmillan and Free Press 1968, p.338.

4 The Great Yorkshire Revival 1792-6: A Study of Mass Revival among the Methodists

John Baxter

Great revivals have taken place in Yorkshire, viz., in Halifax, Leeds, York, Hull and Malton. The political aspect of the present times, excites the minds, and prompts the expectations of many persons, both pious and profane. The Lord sometimes dwells in thick darkness: driving clouds and awful tempest go before him; but his arm shall rule for him.
George Sykes, preacher on the Whitby Station, July 1794[1]

From the reflections I have been led to make on this extraordinary work together with what has taken place throughout Yorkshire, I am led to conclude that this must surely be a prelude to that glorious conquest of Grace, which we are prophetically assured shall take place in the last days; and hence is eminently preparing the way for the grand Millennial Reign of our Redeeming God.
John Moon, preacher in the Sheffield circuit, August 1794[2]

These voices from Yorkshire signalled the height of the psychological climax of one of the most dramatic outbursts of mass revival in the history of the Methodists. This outburst appeared as a unitary phenomenon, a 'burning over' of the Methodist circuits in the North, that began in the West Riding. The phenomenon has remained unobserved despite the particular fascination that the relationship between religious revival and patterns of social-political action has had for contemporary historians and sociologists who have been drawn into renewed debate about the classic Halévy thesis.

E. P. Thompson, building on Halévy's major proposition that Methodism was of critical significance in preventing revolution in late eighteenth- and nineteenth-century England, explained Methodist expansion in the decades following Wesley's death in part by revival growth that appeared as 'a component of the psychic process of counter-revolution'.[3] As a tentative proposition he talked of religious revival 'taking over at the point at which political aspirations met with defeat'.[4] By way of illustration he loosely offered the general occurrence of revival among the Methodists and other sects in the late 1790s. He noted the specific cases of the occurrence of Methodist revival in the Luddite districts after the disturbances of 1811-12 and during 1817 and 1818, the quieter years of post-war popular radicalism, when the Primitive Methodists made headway. Similarly, he observed, the occurrence of revival in the rural counties of the South and East in the aftermath of the 'Swing' riots of 1830-1 was a further illustration.[5] Thus he justified talking of Methodist revival recruitment as the 'chiliasm of despair'.[6]

Thompson further suggested that this pattern was reversible:

> ... whenever hope revived, religious revival was set aside, only to reappear with renewed fervour upon the ruins of the political messianism which had been overthrown.[7]

This pattern of expansion during the period 1790-1832 represented, according to Thompson, 'a pulsation', an 'oscillation' in the social process between 'religious revivalism at the negative, and radical politics (tinged with revolutionary millenarianism) at the positive pole'.[8]

Thompson's speculation, however carefully qualified, has come in for heavy criticism. Hobsbawm, a major critic of the Halévy thesis, had strongly argued that there was a parallel relationship between religious and social-political activity.[9] More recently in his work on the 'Swing' riots, while not relinquishing his position on the Halévy thesis, Hobsbawm's position on the relationship between religious revival and activity appears more reconciled with that of Thompson.[10] While the failure of the promised confrontation of two of the most prominent radical historians may have disappointed conservatives, the 'détente', real or imagined, has not forestalled their attacks on Thompson.[11] Despite Thompson's careful re-statement and qualification of his speculation on the relationship between religious revival and social-political activity,[12] the fact that it is an integral part of a total interpretation which many find unacceptable for purely ideological reasons[13] seems to have made it unworthy of empirical investigation.

Sociologists whose interest in this historical debate relates to attempts to isolate religion as an independent variable in the study of social action have been seemingly better able to prevent their ideological prejudices from distorting their judgment on the state of historical debate. In suggesting to the historian that the key issue to which little strict attention has been paid is chronology, a simple but valuable service has been performed.[14] This article, while confining itself to establishing the historical reality of the appearance of mass revival in the North in the 1790s, attempts primarily to resolve the question of chronology and thus to explore the implications of this continuing controversy.

The 1790s were traumatic years for the Methodist community. The death of Wesley caused an immediate crisis of leadership. Questions that had been long avoided concerning internal organization and the external relation with church and State now had to be answered, not only because the patriarch was dead, but because of external pressure, particularly the demands of loyalty made by the State haunted by the fears of Jacobinism at home and abroad. The Methodists were not able fully to resolve these questions during the decade, as the Kilhamite secession of 1797 forcefully demonstrated.[15] Against the confused background of this 'interregnum' period in the national history of the Methodists, revival appeared in one of the traditional strongholds of Methodism, the West Riding.

The first appearance of revival was seen in the Dewsbury, Birstal and Otley circuits: the Dewsbury preachers claimed its origin there. William Bramwell, stationed in Dewsbury between July 1791 and July 1793, was a determined revivalist preacher who had left the Colne circuit across the Pennines with strong recollections of recent persecution and found Dewsbury no better in his first year there: 'A year of hard labour and much grief', he recalled in his memoirs.[16] John Nelson who arrived in Dewsbury in July 1792 as Bramwell's colleague, reflected on the state of the circuit at that time:

> Things were in such a disagreeable situation, which gave me great concern. Such was the distance between Mr Atlay's people and ours, as I had never witnessed among professors who retained any fear of God. Disputes, hard speeches, and I fear backbiting had soured the minds of many, and took the time that should have been spent in prayer for each other. I was exceedingly tried for the appearance of the people under the Word; and soon wished myself in some other place, so ignorant was I of God.

Nelson consoled his own feeling of inadequacy with a recognition of the determination of Bramwell and a class leader, Ann (Praying Nanny) Cutler, to bring about a revival:

> On one hand Brother Bramwell was pleading with God to restore the broken walls of our Sion, rising about four o'clock in the morning; and on the other Ann Cutler, generally sooner. Between these two it was scarcely possible to be either dead or asleep.[17]

In November 1792 the first signs of revival were recorded in Nelson's memoranda book. Bramwell's pleading and Ann Cutler's house-to-house visits 'to wrestle with God for the people' had begun to take effect. Nelson recorded the numbers 'sanctified' in the revival meetings of the bands, in the classes, at the special watch nights and particularly during the quarterly love feasts in the winter and spring of the following year.[18] The Conference returns for Dewsbury circuit showed a 16% rise in membership over the period July 1792–July 1793, representing a net gain of 90 members.[19] Many more were reached by the revival. John Nelson claimed in March 1793 that 100 new converts had been made in the last three months alone.[20] Such discrepancies can be explained by the impermanence of Methodist conversion, but another piece of evidence suggests a further reason for such discrepancy. In March 1793 when the revival was well established in Dewsbury, William Bramwell claimed they were being visited by people from neighbouring circuits:

> Our love feasts began to be crowded and people from every neighbourhood circuit visited us. Great numbers found pardon and some perfect love. They went home and declared what God had done for them.[21]

Such evidence provides an interesting clue as to the means of transmission of the revival.

In the adjacent Birstal circuit, the revival appears to have broken out early in 1793, through the activities of Thomas Jackson and Robert Smith, the two preachers stationed there.[22] It was perhaps significant that Ann Cutler had visited Birstal in early 1793. Credited by William Bramwell in her obituary with being 'the principal instrument in the beginning of the late revival of the work of God in Yorkshire and Lancashire', her presence dominated the years of revival.[23] That there was an early appearance of revival days in the village of Gomersal in the Birstal circuit is witnessed to by Thomas Pearson, a class leader:

> In the year 1793, at the commencement of the late war (February 1793),

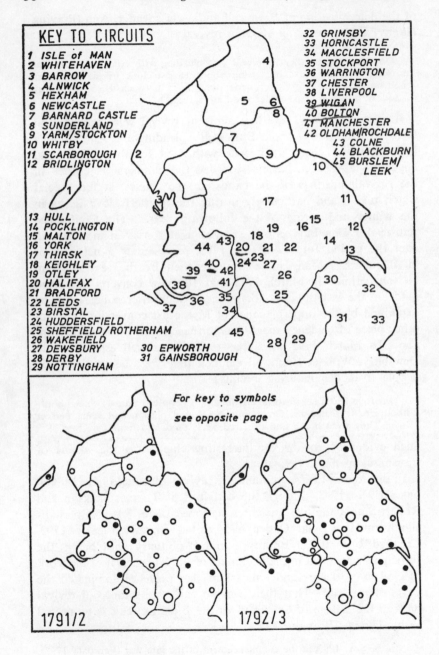

KEY TO CIRCUITS

1 ISLE of MAN
2 WHITEHAVEN
3 BARROW
4 ALNWICK
5 HEXHAM
6 NEWCASTLE
7 BARNARD CASTLE
8 SUNDERLAND
9 YARM/STOCKTON
10 WHITBY
11 SCARBOROUGH
12 BRIDLINGTON

13 HULL
14 POCKLINGTON
15 MALTON
16 YORK
17 THIRSK
18 KEIGHLEY
19 OTLEY
20 HALIFAX
21 BRADFORD
22 LEEDS
23 BIRSTAL
24 HUDDERSFIELD
25 SHEFFIELD/ROTHERHAM
26 WAKEFIELD
27 DEWSBURY
28 DERBY
29 NOTTINGHAM

30 EPWORTH
31 GAINSBOROUGH

32 GRIMSBY
33 HORNCASTLE
34 MACCLESFIELD
35 STOCKPORT
36 WARRINGTON
37 CHESTER
38 LIVERPOOL
39 WIGAN
40 BOLTON
41 MANCHESTER
42 OLDHAM/ROCHDALE
43 COLNE
44 BLACKBURN
45 BURSLEM/
   LEEK

For key to symbols
see opposite page

1791/2

1792/3

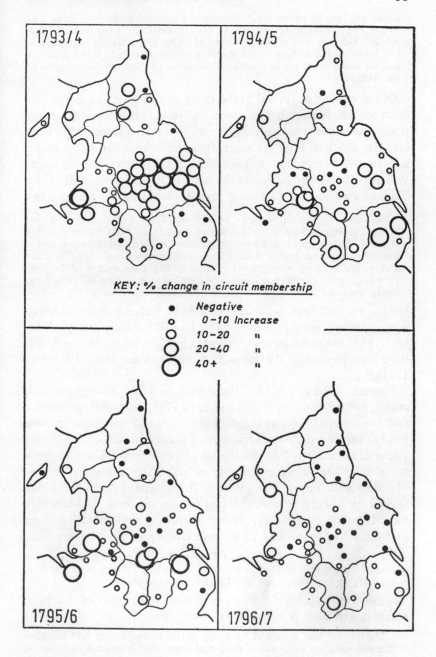

KEY: % change in circuit membership

● Negative
○ 0-10 Increase
○ 10-20 "
○ 20-40 "
○ 40+ "

a day was appointed by the Government to be set aside for fasting and prayer. In consequence of which, prayer meetings were held in our village. Religion was at a very low ebb. The first meeting was held in our house at five o'clock in the morning. Many attended: and no sooner had we commenced the service than the power of God manifestly affected the assembly.[24]

Of the coming of revival to the Otley circuit little is known. The influence of Elizabeth Dickinson, a young Bingley girl whose trances were drawing thousands to prayer meetings, may have been felt. Her death in 1793 cut short what might have become a major role in the events that followed.[25] To the Birstal circuit came William Bramwell appointed as circuit preacher in July 1793. Thomas Pearson, the Gomersal class leader, recalled his coming:

> He came to us full of faith and of the Holy Ghost. His powerful preaching and fervent prayers were so mighty through faith, that the stoutest-hearted sinner trembled under him. Before that time we had a partial outpouring, but a mighty shower then descended, and the truth and power of God wonderfully prevailed. My class increased to sixty members, and all ranks and degrees of men began to attend the preaching. Every place of worship in the neighbourhood was crowded.[26]

During his first year in the circuit a 58% increase in membership was recorded following on a 14% increase during the previous year. This dramatic success was matched elsewhere in the Yorkshire circuits during the same Conference Year (July 1793–July 1794).[27]

Success, however, earned Bramwell and his colleagues their critics. In the Dewsbury circuit earlier in 1793, Bramwell and Nelson had encountered popular resistance to revivalist meetings. In June 1793 at Gawthorpe, youths had stoned the roof of the chapel during a revivalist meeting.[28] In the Birstal circuit Bramwell was facing a more articulate set of critics who attacked the 'enthusiast' nature of Methodist conversion. Bramwell successfully defended the revival as a work of divine inception against such critics within the Methodist community. Thomas Growth, a Gomersal clothier and class leader testified to the overcoming of his doubts:

> In the love feast on Christmas Day (1793), I had such a conviction that this work was of God as caused me to close in with it and give it, not only my approval, but my heartiest co-operation.[29]

Thomas Pearson, his fellow class leader, talked too of a critical reaction and how it came to be overcome:

> The revival was esteemed by many to be extraordinary and singular. Some thought the work was of God, and others that it was too enthusiastic.

But it often happened that when the persons who had imbibed the latter opinion went to hear for themselves, the divine power affected them and they were constrained to cry aloud to God for mercy.[30]

By July 1793 the revival had reached the Bradford circuit, testified Jonothan Saville, a warper and class leader, describing his role as a humble lay-revivalist:

> I used to go after I had finished my work for the day, sometimes as far as Lindley and all arounds, to prayer meetings, and then would come home at midnight, sleep in the wool at the mill, then up in the morning to my work.[31]

But the revival must have come to Bradford earlier. In the Halifax circuit, where the revival was dated from the Greetland love feast of June 1793, Robert Lomas the preacher bore testimony to the presence of visitors from Bradford who had already experienced the coming of the revival. From Greetland, Lomas recorded, the revival spread throughout the Halifax circuit in the winter of 1793-4.[32] Joseph Entwisle, a preacher in the Leeds circuit, visited Halifax in February 1794 and noted:

> The Lord has poured out his spirit plenteously in the Halifax circuit. They have added upwards of three hundred new members the last quarter: most of whom, so far as they can judge at present are justified. Their meetings are frequently noisy and long continued, often till midnight, frequently till morning. It is not unusual for persons to be crying out in distress in various parts of the chapel, and others praying for them. Now a number of stout fellows, kneeling around a sinner in distress, cry aloud, 'Come Lord Jesus, come quickly'. Anon, the captive being set free, they seem to shake the very house with crying, 'Glory be to God'. The noise and confusion sometimes are very great, and one could wish it otherwise; yet, as the preachers see hundreds of sinners turning from the error of their ways, they say little to put a stop to it.[33]

From the Hull circuit in the East Riding Alexander Mather, the circuit preacher, observed the progress of the revival in the West Riding circuits and commented on its effect on the Hull society in December 1793:

> When we heard of the great outpourings of the Grace of God upon the circuits of the West Riding of Yorkshire, where hundreds, even thousands have lately been awakened and converted, a very earnest desire was kindled in the heart of the people, especially among the leaders, for a revival in our society.

Unfulfilled prayers for revival days led Mather to reflect on the presence of 'inhibitions' which he described as a 'too anxious attachment to decorum and order, an aversion to loud lamentation and cries in the public congregation'.[34] However at the Christmas love feast of 1793 and in successive prayer meetings the revival came to Hull and spread throughout the East Riding circuits.[35]

In the winter months of 1793-4 the revival fires blazed in the heart of the West Riding. Ann Cutler had visited many of the circuits there. Her 'ministry', which was based on Dewsbury, had taken her to the Birstal, Otley and Bradford circuits in 1793. Early in 1794 she turned her attention to the Leeds circuit where Bramwell her biographer claimed, 'though vital religion had been very low, the Lord made use of her at the beginning of the revival'.[36] George Wood, a preacher in the Wakefield circuit, made no mention of her visit when he traced the origin of the revival in the Leeds circuit to a prayer meeting held at Woodhouse in February 1794.[37] Neither did Joseph Entwisle mention her when describing his day-to-day experiences as a preacher in the Leeds circuit. His entry in his memoranda book for 9 February noted:

> Preached at Horsforth this morning. The Society here is in a remarkably dead state. I endeavoured to speak with the utmost plainness, both in the sermon and in the society. But God alone can revive his work. Preached at Woodhouse at noon. Here the scene was quite different. The Lord is pouring out his Spirit in a very extraordinary manner. Almost all the inhabitants of the village appear to be under a religious concern. They have been praying night and day most of the week, generally continuing together from evening till morning. As far as we can judge, great numbers are flocking to Christ.[38]

His entry for 16 February described the Woodhouse events in greater detail:

> One meeting, held about a fortnight ago, was remarkable. A number of people were assembled in expectation of a prayer meeting. It happened, however, that none of the persons who exercise on such occasions attended. After they had sat in silence for a considerable time, a poor woman fell upon her knees, and with an extraordinary loud and bitter cry, pleaded for mercy. While she continued crying, 'God be merciful to me a sinner', some of the company went out, and called upon one or two of the leaders, who came and held a meeting; in which several were brought into the liberty of the children of God.[39]

During the first two weeks of February Entwisle recorded similar experiences at Scarcroft, Harwood, Chapeltown and Belisle in the Leeds circuit. His description of the events at the latter place emphasized his distaste for the 'enthusiast' nature of current events.

> Our warm friends from Woodhouse were there: they had gone beyond all bounds of decency, such screaming and bawling I never heard. Divided into small companies in different parts of the chapel, some singing, others

praying, others praising, clapping of hands, etc, all was confusion and uproar. I was struck with amazement and consternation. What to do I could not tell. However, as there appeared to be no possibility of breaking up the meeting, I quietly withdrew. They continued thus until five o'clock in the morning. What shall I say to these things? I believe God is working very powerfully on the minds of many; but I think Satan, or, at least, *the animal nature*, has a great hand in all this.[40]

On the 16 February a more magnanimous spirit prevailed in his writing. Entwisle talked of the 'good work going on with amazing rapidity in Birstal, Dewsbury, Bradford and Keighley circuits'.[41] This spirit was sustained in his accounts of the spread of revival throughout the Leeds circuit in the spring and summer months of 1794.[42] Describing his participation at a meeting held in a barn in Harwood for the people of the surrounding villages in June, Entwisle, so cold towards the new 'enthusiasm' four months previously, confessed:

... my heart overflowed with joy, I went out of the common way and gave out two verses of a hymn in the middle of a sermon.[43]

The revival fire raged on southwards from Leeds to the Wakefield circuit. Here at a watchnight in February 1794, George Wood recorded, 'the Lord began his work in Wakefield in a manner we had not seen before'. He related this to the events in the Leeds circuit:

There has been a great ingathering in every place since the last Conference (July 1793), but more so since the third of February last, when our friends at Woodhouse met together for a prayer meeting.[44]

In the southernmost circuit of the West Riding, Sheffield, the revival appeared first at the Lady Day love feast (March 1794). John Moon one of the preachers testified in a letter to T. Coke (from which the following quotations are taken):

The presence and power of God were unusually felt, and there was a cry amongst the people, but it was not attended with even the appearance of disorder. From this time the work went swiftly on.

In June, however, the Sheffield revival realized a new intensity. Moon's testimony is quoted in full to give a more vital impression of the revivalists at work and to convey the psychic drama of revival:

At the last quarterly love feast, the fire broke out in a more extraordinary and amazing manner. The meeting began with its usual calmness and order, and so continued till we were about to conclude. But while we thought thereon, a person came and requested our prayers for one in deep distress. Soon after the same request was repeated for a woman in the gallery. I then desired two or three of the local preachers to go and pray with her; intending to keep my place and conduct the remaining part of the meeting with all possible decorum. It being however a new thing, and to them not a little strange, they appeared reluctant to go. I knew not what to do, I hesitated for a moment, but the cry of the distressed still prevailing, *I determined to sacrifice regularity to the season of usefulness* which presented itself to me. I therefore went up into the gallery and prayed with the afflicted persons.

Moon received 'no answer' because, he thought, of 'my reluctance to engage'. One of the local preachers took the initiative. Below on the floor of the chapel this man 'gave out a hymn and prayed'. Then came the frenzy. Moon recalled:

> ... and now the power of God in a wonderful manner filled the place. The cries of the distressed instantly broke out like a clap of thunder from every part of the chapel and lost the voice of prayer.

Local preachers spread out to pray and give comfort to the afflicted. Moon, the reluctant revivalist, exclaimed:

> I never saw anything like it. It could not but appear to the idle spectator all confusion but to those engaged there, it was glorious regularity.[45]

Henry Longden, a merchant and ironmaster and also a class leader, corroborated this:

> Mr Moon called upon one of the local preachers to pray. While he was pleading with God; he was carried out of himself with Holy fervour, in an extraordinary manner. The spirit of God came as a mighty rushing wind and filled the place where they were assembled, and overwhelmed every individual by its powerful influence. A few who did not understand it, and resisted it, were confounded and in their terror escaped as if for their lives. There was presently a loud and bitter cry in every part of the chapel.[46]

Over one hundred persons were 'saved' on this and two successive nights. Crowds assembled at the door of the chapel to witness the events and on the first two nights they were admitted. On the third night, a hostile crowd assembled at this scene of what was popularly designated 'Methodist madness' and twenty constables were called in to keep order.[47]

The revival fire raged on throughout the Sheffield circuit and the other West Riding circuits in the summer and autumn of 1794 and had begun to take hold in the East Riding. John Nelson, travelling south from Dewsbury in the autumn, recorded the work going on at Rothwell, midway between Leeds and Wakefield. He passed through Sheffield and reached Derby in August where he met the bands assembled to pray for revival. In October on his return north he witnessed the revival now taking hold in Derby-shire at Belper[48] : it had spread westwards as well as southwards and eastwards. By the winter of 1794 a ring of circuits around the West Riding were affected by the revival. The circuits covering the North and East Ridings, Lincolnshire, Derbyshire, Staffordshire, Cheshire and Lancashire were experiencing the revival. Ann Cutler arrived in Derby in December 1794, having followed her itinerant calling across the Pennines, through her native Lancashire and into Cheshire and Staffordshire during the previous two months. She described her exertions in Lancashire, particularly in her letters from Oldham and Manchester which date the outbreak of the revival there. From Derby she travelled on to Macclesfield where she arrived on 15 December seriously ill; on the 29 she died.[49]

The intensity of the revival was sustained into 1795 throughout the 'burned over' districts of 1794. Its intensity diminished in the circuits which had first experienced revival but the work continued in the southern West Riding circuits into 1796. In the Sheffield circuit the revival was sustained the longest. It is significant that William Bramwell was appointed to this circuit in July 1795. His sense of mission was never stronger[50] and his success was consider-able. In the winter of 1795 while engaged in bringing the revival to the rural south of the circuit in North Derbyshire he paused to reflect:

> This has been the greatest labour I have yet experienced. The last Sunday both chapels (in Sheffield) were filled and at Garden Street after preaching, the power of God descended and a cry went through the gallery ... I left many in distress.[51]

Bramwell's correspondence indicated the work continuing as late as September 1796.[52] The fire of revival was dying down through 1796 although it continued to progress southwards into the Mid-lands. The heat had gone out of the fire.

In seeking explanations of these events it should at once be recog-nized that mass revival was a characteristic form of Methodist expansion. A recent interpretation of the development of Metho-dism in Cornwall, an area in some ways similar to Yorkshire in that Methodism was a major cultural factor, suggests that periods of mass revival occurred at intervals of sixteen to eighteen years, appearing as a natural, 'generational' pattern of renewal and expansion.[53] Mass revival, at least in the Cornish experience, may not demand any further explanation. While what occurred between 1792-6 in Yorkshire and the bordering counties may have been part of a similar 'generational' pattern, its magnitude and particular timing suggest the existence of other factors at work.

The question of precipitating factors can be approached on two levels. The evidence suggests the revival had its own internal social and psychological dynamics which contributed to mass revival on such a dramatic scale. However, the revival did not occur in a vacuum. Some attempt must be made to relate it to the wider social context.

Any attempt to discover the revival's inner dynamics cannot ignore the bias of the descriptive evidence. Virtually all the testimonies were made by those committed to the revival. Even the preachers who were sceptical of its divine inspiration and who were embarrassed by its noisy 'enthusiasm' were swept along by its powerful current. It was left to enemies outside the Methodist community to accuse the Methodists of deliberate manipulation. The validity of these charges increases when the particular definition of the initial doubts of several of the Methodist preachers is borne in mind. It is difficult to prove, given the limitations of historical evidence, the existence of neuro-physiological mechanics of manipulated conversion induced by the revivalists.[54] Nevertheless, their existence should not be discounted.

The suggestion that the revival was precipitated by internal social and psychological dynamics deriving from particular events taking place within the Methodist community comes from involved, committed observers. Their descriptions of a critical preliminary phase to revival, such as that of John Nelson of Dewsbury who talked of 'a time when discipline had been strictly attended to',[55] do not easily lend themselves to interpretation. Yet the appearance of revival following on a period of intense 'seriousness', usually a response to some crisis (initially an internal one in the case of the Dewsbury circuit where the Methodist community had been torn apart by a dispute over Wesley's right to appoint preachers over the heads of the local trustees during 1788-90[56]), seems to have been characteristic. The fact of Wesley's death in March 1791 was critical in precipitating deep-rooted organizational crisis throughout the Methodist community nationally. Joseph Entwisle, stationed in the Halifax circuit, reacted to the news with apprehension echoed throughout the Methodist world:

My soul trembles for the ark of the Lord. There are men of so many different judgments in our connexion, all of whom now claim an equal authority, especially the senior preachers, that I fear we may have some division among us.[57]

It was a time above all when growth and renewal could help to unite a movement threatened with breakdown. During the period of intense introspection among the Methodist community following Wesley's death, a desire for revival was generated among a section of the committed. This desire was expressed in the mental and physical self-denying ritual of those who prayed for revival at Dewsbury where particular local factors were also at work. Such activity among the preachers and local leaders seems to have dominated the typical revival drama throughout the northern circuits after the events at Dewsbury had taken place. As the reports of events such as those at Dewsbury and Woodhouse were transmitted they contributed to the generation of expectation seemingly fulfilled or self-fulfilled in the frenzy of revival days.

Not merely report but the actual presence of seemingly charismatic figures such as William Bramwell and Ann Cutler may have been a critical determinant of the pattern of revival. Bramwell, whose stature grew throughout these years of revival when he was stationed in three West Riding circuits, was by 1795 being acclaimed an 'angel' by the superstitious Derbyshire folk because they had witnessed a 'miracle' preceding his arrival.[58] Similarly Ann Cutler's itinerancy coincided remarkably with the chronology of the revival.

It would be in the actual drama of the revival meeting that the neuro-physiological mechanics of a manipulated conversion process operated. It is in the descriptions of the victims, such as that of George Wood's of the Wakefield converted of 1794, that the effects of the revivalist's onslaught can best begun to be appreciated:

Some have been in the society for many years, others have heard the preaching a few times and many had no concern till the moment they were cut to the heart with a powerful sense of their lost condition. In some the distress was great, the anguish of spirit affecting the body, and drops of sweat issued from every pore; in others there was no remarkable terror, but a consciousness of want of divine faith and love. Sometimes they continued an hour or two without any deliverance, but many were enabled to believe much sooner. Those that are brought through much distress, are generally led into a calm awaiting in hope a few minutes before they are delivered from their guilt, and then in a moment break forth in praise and thanksgiving. These frequently discover a peculiar tender sympathy with those who remain in distress, an ardent love and gratitude to those who prayed with them, and, almost universally, a deep concern for their unconverted relations.[59]

John Moon had witnessed a similar transformation in the Sheffield victims of June 1794:

> ...though sunk in the deepest distress, and crying out under the bitterest anguish; yet when the Comforter came, their faces shone with holy joy, and their eyes sparkled with divine rapture.[60]

The characteristic description of the revival meeting conveys the highly charged, hysterical moment of conversion. It suggests the operation of certain social and psychological mechanisms for which it is tempting to use terms like 'crowd contagion' and 'self-inducement' to attempt to add analytical depth to pure narrative. If the evidence is limited, where it is available, it is highly suggestive. Reference to the presence of children among the 'saved' is frequent and highly significant.[61] Parents brought their children to meetings. Accompanied by one or both parents who might have already been reached by the message, the child was not only extremely vulnerable to the revivalist's message but also to the highly charged emotional atmosphere. John Moon, in noting the exceptional participation of children during the revival in the Sheffield circuit, described what would appear to be the extremes of 'self-inducement':

> Even little boys and girls have now prayer meetings among themselves; and one company of lads meets constantly in a field, in the evening when the weather is fine; they form a circle, and pray for each other, till they have some signal and answer of divine approbation.[62]

An awareness of the wider social context is fundamental to an explanation of the revival. This is of limited value unless the attraction of the revivalist's message can be appreciated. For those who sought comfort from the world the revivalist could offer more than the temporary emotional release provided by a cathartic conversion. For many the conversion was a 'new birth', the offer and the receipt of a new identity and a new confidence. A recent convert to the Sheffield revival of June 1794 testified:

> The Almighty has sent down the offer of the present revival as a cure for every evil. When the soul is truly alive to God, every external disorder will be rectified.[63]

The promise of a lasting sense of emotional reassurance for 'this life' and the hope for 'after life' in reward for the dutiful submission to the pains of 'this world' could be sustained for many in the close-knit association of the Methodist community where both social identity for the lonely and insecure and material comfort for the poor and hungry was provided. Whatever way the revivalist's message was conceived through individual experience in the heat of the revival drama, it is not difficult, in examining the social context of the revival, to understand why many of the audience should be there to seek some sort of emotional reassurance.

Throughout the 'burned over' district of 1792-6, soaring statistics of unemployment, prices and poor law expenditure[64] were translated into the social reality of market disturbances and labour disputes. 1795, a year of near famine and widespread market disturbances in the North, witnessed in at least one of the largest industrial communities of the West Riding, the presence of no less than five major apocalyptic signs; war, pestilence, famine, flooding and an earthquake![65] Such signs made the overtures to popular credulity of Richard Brothers, London's 'mad' prophet, in 1795 seem far less absurd in provincial centres where it seems he was extending his search for the 'lost tribes'.[66]

The real impact of economic dislocation created by the war was perhaps not felt until the revival had developed its early momentum, but its appearance intensified feelings of frustration and anxiety among working people in the northern counties, who were beginning to feel the effects of certain structural changes at work in their industries. This was true of both the woollen industry of the northern West Riding and the cutlery and metal working industries of the southern West Riding.[67] Unemployment drove men in despair into enlisting in the army. The womenfolk, deserted by husbands, sons and sweethearts, in need of spiritual as well as material comfort were extremely vulnerable to the revivalist's promise.[68]

Economic dislocation was matched in many communities by political unrest. The first moment of popular radicalism which occurred in the early 1790s has been examined in depth by several recent historians,[69] notably E. P. Thompson, who used its appearance and submersion in the following years of repression in the wake of Methodist and wider revivalist recruitment as justification for talking of a pattern of oscillation between radical politics and religious revival.[70] Currie and Hartwell, the keenest critics of Thompson's interpretation of Methodism, have asked some penetrating questions about this oscillation:

Does the whole population oscillate first to political action, then when it fails, to religious? Or does one section of the population oscillate to political action and a second to religious when the first is disappointed? In either case the oscillation should leave some mark on Methodism.[71]

Thompson quite rightly replies that both patterns can be present but neither are universal.[72] Any assessment of the pattern Thompson offers as a 'tentative suggestion' must involve an awareness of the relative strength of radical activity in particular communities in the North. The existence of popular radical activity appears to be something about which Currie and Hartwell know very little. Nevertheless, they are confident in their total rejection of Thompson's ideas:

> The growth rate of Methodism as a whole and in the northern counties in particular, shows no significant association between repression or failure of political activity and the expansion of Methodism.[73]

When the evidence for the 1790s is fully assembled it bears out Thompson's speculation. *Why do we believe this?*

Popular radical clubs had appeared by late 1791 and early 1792 in many communities in the North; Manchester, Liverpool, Warrington and Newton in Lancashire, Stockport and Chester in Cheshire, Sheffield and Wakefield in the West Riding and Barnard Castle in Durham. Below the level of organized activity was a general upsurge of excitement, spreading at obscure levels with rising expectation of imminent change, associated especially from late 1791 to late 1792 with the works of Tom Paine, with talk of equality and the 'Rights of Man'. Against this background appeared the counter drama of repression. Following the Royal Proclamation of May 1792 the mobilization of the forces of loyalism proceeded, gaining strength throughout the year in reaction to developments in France. The loyalist backlash climaxed in the winter of 1792-3 in an orgy of 'Paine burnings', presentation of addresses of loyalty and local prosecutions of radicals, stage-managed by local branches of the Reeves Association. The declaration of war in February 1793 helped to recycle popular aspirations into patriotic fervour. The radical clubs were driven underground. By March 1793 only the Stockport and Sheffield clubs continued to issue public statements. New clubs were formed early in 1793 in the West Riding and Midlands but were never able to hold public meetings in their communities without attracting the unwelcome attentions of the local agencies of church and King.[74]

Yes but were the same people involved?

With the onset of repression came the revival. To William Bramwell, the veteran revivalist, its coming seemed to have been a purgation:

> The Lord saw that, in Yorkshire, we were in too great a union with the world, which had certainly been the case for a number of years. He now drew the line and to His name be ascribed the wisdom and glory.[75]

While there is little direct evidence of the conscious organization of a counter-active movement by the preachers, many like George Sykes on the Whitby station in 1794 regarded the 'political aspect' of the times as a danger to the established order both within the Methodist community and in the wider society. This fear was not expressed simply in rigid conformity to Wesley's 'no politics' maxim but more fundamentally in the moulding of the ideological conservatism found in the Wesleyan Connexion after the secession of the more liberal elements as the Kilhamites in 1797. A minority *few* of the preachers who felt sympathetic towards popular political aspirations created a general suspicion about the loyalty of the Methodists. In response to this the Methodist hierarchy responded as early as 1793 by issuing loyalist statements and propaganda literature.[76] Many of this minority were forced into conformity with the official view but played no active role as agents of counter-revolution. This could be based on sound pragmatism such as that shown by Joseph Entwisle in the Leeds circuit in 1792, who, realizing the antagonisms within his own congregation, decided, 'least said, soonest mended'.[77] It could also be rooted in fear of the church and King mob. Thomas Taylor related his experience of Bolton in 1793:

> I came in very great hopes of peace and quietness. But numbers in the town were almost intoxicated by what they pretended to be loyalty; and all who would not drink and swear, and curse the French, were deemed disaffected to the government. I fell under condemnation for the above reasons.[78]

If there is no talk by observers of the revival feeding off repression, the association of the appearance of revival and counter-revolution is implicit in Bramwell's talk of the revival being the means of terminating 'a union with the world' and in the extravagant language of George Sykes, the Whitby preacher, witnessing the climax of the revival in Yorkshire:

> Judgment may shortly begin at the house of God. The royal sceptre may be broken – the pompous mitre be profaned and thrown to the

ground – and the idols be cast to the moles and to the bats. Their possessors may have to go, in the clefts of the rocks, and into the tops of the ragged rocks, for fear of the Lord, and for the glory of his Majesty, when he ariseth to shake terribly the earth.[79]

Currie and Hartwell's claim of there being 'no significant association between repression or failure of political activity and the expansion of Methodism' is highly questionable, at least when applied to the 1790s.

An examination of the evidence relating to the Sheffield circuit, where the radical cause was stronger than anywhere else in the North, reveals an extraordinary coincidence in the appearance of revival and the onset of repression. Of particular value in the case of the Sheffield circuit is the wealth of material that makes it possible to examine the idea of individual and collective oscillation between radicalism and 'enthusiastic' religion.

In Sheffield, with a population of 30,000, a weak local elite and the absence of a church and King mob contributed to a high degree of popular radical mobilization in the town and surrounding villages. The self-styled Sheffield 'sans culottes' had danced in the streets to celebrate the French victories at Jenappes and Valmy in late 1792: crowds of 6,000 were reported.[80] A radical artisan vanguard, organized as the Sheffield Society for Constitutional Information was claimed to have a 'ticket' membership of 2,500 in mid 1792.[81] At the height of its activities in mid 1793, a petition containing 8,000 signatures was sent to parliament to demand reform.[82] Radical propaganda centred on the press of a newspaper publisher, Joseph Gales, and on the 'missionary' work of lecturers. As a result of their work, radical clubs were organized at Leeds in the West Riding, and Birmingham and Coventry in the Midlands.[83]

The Government's active concern for their activities began with the arrest of the Sheffield and Leeds delegate to the Scottish Convention in December 1793[84] and ended with the break-up of the leadership group and their propaganda machine with the arrest and flight of the leading activists in May and June 1794.[85] While during the last six months of the society's existence there was a drastic falling off in membership, coinciding with a 'left-ward' shift in policy,[86] the society drew huge crowds to its public meetings in February and April 1794.[87] The arrests of May and June forestalled their hopes for an English Convention.[88] Overnight church and King became legitimized in Sheffield and were institutionalized in the Sheffield Loyal Independent Volunteers under government licence as the local men of property took heart.[89] That same June the climax of the first moment of Methodist revival was reached in Sheffield. At the moment that the hopes of popular radicalism were finally extinguished, religious revival burst into flame. The power of the revival in the autumn of 1794 appeared to serve as a warning of the imminence of the millennium to serious observers throughout the West Riding.[90] Such phenomena as the visions described in a report in the *Sheffield Iris* of 7 August 1794 were symptomatic of the disturbed psychological state of the revival districts. Under the heading, 'Age of Nonsense' appeared the following:

> On Monday last a most astonishing phenomenon was seen in the heavens by many credible or as some folks say, credulous eye witnesses … A man on horseback in an armoured cap and cape appeared galloping about in a disk of sun, but lo suddenly two martial figures attacked him and cut off his head.[91]

There was some resurgence of the radical cause following the acquittals in the State Trials and the return of the Sheffield leaders from their detention in London in December 1794.[92] While public meetings were held in Sheffield throughout 1795 until curtailed by the passing of the Two Acts,[93] the radical cause was being driven underground by the new climate of repression. For the 'sub-political' and uncommitted who in Sheffield had formed the large crowds at meetings held by the SSCI throughout the years 1792-4, the 'mad Methodists' may momentarily have offered an attractive view of an alternative millennium to that offered them by the political visionaries of the SSCI, particularly during the autumn of repression of 1794. The link cannot be forged with complete certainty, but it is not inconceivable that some measure of oscillation between radical politics and 'enthusiast' revivalist religious activity took place and that this contributed to the intensity of the revival. That there was a resurgence in radical politics not only in Sheffield but elsewhere in the West Riding in 1795 in no way contradicts the idea of oscillation because the power of revival was waning at its original source. In the Leeds circuit where there was renewed popular political activity on a scale unknown before in 1795, the revival had burnt itself out by November 1794.[94]

An investigation of the religious associations of the leadership group of the SSCI, the only such group in the North that it is possible with existing evidence to investigate, reveals evidence of individual oscillation. The Methodists had provided a location for some of the radical vanguard before as well as during the revival years. Similiar evidence of Methodists associated with radical politics in the West Riding comes from Halifax and Wakefield.[95] It was still possible for the Methodist radical to reconcile the demands imposed by his religious and political associations in the early 1790s. Among thirty committee members of the SSCI between 1791-4, the following seven were found from Methodist circuit class lists[96] to have had association at some time with the Methodists:

Committee Members of the SSCI and their record of association[97]
with the Methodists

Name and Committee role	Membership of Sheffield Methodist Society recorded for month of June (x denotes member)							
	1789	1790	1792	1793	1794	1795	1796	1799
Richard Beale (shopkeeper) Secret Committee March 1794	x	x	x	x	x	x	x	
William Broomhead (cutler) Secretary Nov 1793–May 1794						x		
John Grainger (———) Committee of July 1794							x	x
Henry Hill (shoe knife forger) Founding Committee 1791-2	x	x		x	x	x	x	
Edward Oakes (silver plater) Committee Feb–March 1794	x	x	x		x	x	x	
James Watson (———) Committee of July 1794						x		
George Kent (scissor manu- facturer) Committee Feb–March 1794				x	x	x	x	

Three of the above had associations with the Methodists reaching back into the 1780s. Hill, one of the founders of the SSCI, claimed to have left the society after one year yet was making arms for them in 1794.[98] Beale was an active member of the leadership throughout 1792-4. Oakes was active in the early part of 1794, his vitriolic 'Sermon on the Fast Day' was delivered by him to a 6,000 crowd at the mass meeting the SSCI held in February 1794.[99]

All three left the Old Connexion in the 1797 secession, in the cases of Beale and Oakes to become preachers with the Kilhamite 'Tom Paine' Methodists.[100] Both Hill and Oakes' records of association with the Methodists suggest some measure of individual oscillation for neither's name appears in the class lists at the periods of their most significant political activism. The reason for their absence must be sought in the question of individual conscience. In view of Beale's consistent record it is unlikely that internal disciplinary processes operated in the Methodist community. Three of the four remaining committee members with Methodist associations were not found in the class lists until June 1796, their appearance reflecting perhaps the existence of a wider pattern of mass oscillation between radical politics and revivalist religion.

For one of these three there is some interesting supporting evidence. William Broomhead, a cutler from whom the war had taken his livelihood, had been a member of the SSCI in its early days. His advocacy of physical force had led to his expulsion, but he returned as full-time secretary during the 'left-ward swing' of 1793-4. Presiding at a public meeting of the SSCI in December 1793, Broomhead was described by the loyalist press as

... an apology for a human creature, this cameleon, this changeling, who has attempted to try all the religions in Sheffield.[101]

Here indeed was raw material for the Methodist revivalists. Broomhead, a broken man after his arrest in May 1794 and subsequent detention in London until December 1794, returned to Sheffield to find refuge with the Methodists. Other examples outside the leadership group can be cited with less confidence, but the case of Joseph Mather, the Jacobin street entertainer who ended his days among the Methodists writing devotional works, was strikingly similar to Broomhead's.[102] That this refuge was only temporary is indicated by the fact that Broomhead and five others of the seven SSCI veterans who were members of the Methodist society in 1796 deserted between 1796-9, possibly all following Beale and Oakes' example and joining the Kilhamites. Their association with the Methodist society may not have meant a total sublimation of their radical consciousness during the years of counter-revolution but the Kilhamite community offered a milieu in which that consciousness could be re-born.[103]

Whether such examples can be said to represent a mirocosm of

wider patterns of mass oscillation is questionable. Evidence relating
to the most politically active does not have to be representative
of mass behaviour. All that can be said of those whose radical
convictions were less sure – those among the 'sub-political' mass
who had been awakened in the early 1790s – is that the loss of
such leadership as the SSCI had provided left them alone, vulnerable to the tender mercies of the Wesleyan priesthood which was
increasingly becoming the tool of counter-revolution.[104]

While it may never be possible to discover to what extent
'oscillation' was a real social and psychological process, and to
what extent, if any, it contributed to the momentum of religious
revival in the 1790s, there is at least enough evidence to consider
Thompson's 'constructive speculation' a worthwhile exercise.

This point established, it should not be denied that other factors,
possibly far more important ones, influenced the momentum of
the revival. The internal social and psychological dynamics of the
revival itself, while they remain largely obscure, were important.
The impact of external social and psychological processes other
than those associated with political repression, particularly those
created by economic dislocation, were also of significance.

Of necessity some parts of our explanation appear speculative
and final conclusions unambitious. It must be recognized that in
the way that it has been recorded from a historical viewpoint,
religious behaviour (like many other areas of human experience)
does not always lend itself to open inquiry. Nevertheless, a full
investigation of the whole range of historical evidence relating to
such phenomenon should be made in order to come closer to
understanding it as historical reality. This is what has been
attempted here.

Appendix

Membership of Methodist Circuits in the North 1790-7

(returns to July Conference)

Yorkshire (West Riding)	1790	1791	1792	1793	1794	1795	1796	1797
Keighley	1,480	900	990	1,020	1,400	1,360	1,420	1,400
Otley		560	549	690	1,200	1,100	1,300	1,100
Bradford	1,085	1,095	1,170	1,180	1,400	1,430	1,460	1,476
Halifax	1,111	1,115	1,124	1,103	1,500	1,500	1,600	1,706
Leeds	2,157	2,080	2,100	2,120	3,400	3,450	2,640	2,460
Birstal	1,266	1,230	720	820	1,300	1,400	1,200	1,070
Dewsbury			540	630	780	820	752	611
Huddersfield	846	780	760	830	1,190	1,286	1,600	1,700
Wakefield	706	730	744	770	1,050	1,080	1,500	950
Sheffield	1,690	1,690	1,700	1,661	1,370	1,750	3,000	3,261
Rotherham					563	637	800	820
Total	10,341	10,180	10,397	10,824	15,153	15,813	17,272	16,559

Yorkshire (East Riding)

	1790	1791	1792	1793	1794	1795	1796	1797
Pocklington	830	834	463	466	740	940	800	760
Hull	665	664	663	640	1,200	1,280	1,290	1,200
Bridlington			350	354	450	450	500	477
Total	1,495	1,498	1,476	1,460	2,390	2,670	2,590	2,437

Yorkshire (North Riding)

	1790	1791	1792	1793	1794	1795	1796	1797
Scarborough	652	621	607	633	800	500	530	550
Malton						730	760	720
Whitby	482	545	514	517	515	530	526	513
Thirsk	674	629	641	643	828	978	1,140	1,280
Yarm/Stockton	525	554	580	591	620	625	670	640
Total	2,333	2,349	2,342	2,384	2,763	3,363	3,526	3,703
Yorkshire (York)	880	874	879	890	1,300	1,220	1,214	1,229

Lancashire

Manchester	2,060	2,090	1,400	1,500	1,850	3,300	2,322	2,400
Oldham			793	826	900	1,070	800	950
Bolton	1,152	1,160	1,220	1,172	870	1,080	1,150	1,260
Wigan					360	430	606	580
Rochdale							780	950
Liverpool	1,020	1,050	660	666	963	982	1,000	1,123
Warrington/ Northwich			475	448	538	624	678	720
Blackburn	930	955	1,040	1,090	1,180	993	870	890
Colne	976	1,020	1,010	1,030	1,080	1,120	1,076	1,180
Lancaster						53	230	350
Barrow								560
Total	6,138	6,275	6,598	6,732	7,741	9,652	9,512	10,963

Northumberland and Durham

Newcastle	700	780	800	800	740	800	860	846
Alnwick	290	300	350	320	300	320	280	202
Hexham	980	986	620	650	820	789	660	750
Sunderland	1,300	1,250	1,154	1,064	1,090	1,028	980	960
Barnard Castle			383	400	554	560	452	438
Total	3,270	3,316	3,307	3,234	3,504	3,497	3,632	3,196

Cumberland and Westmorland

Whitehaven	302	282	288	300	350	400	401	403
Isle of Man	2,580	2,500	2,400	2,330	2,430	2,433	2,433	2,750

Economic Indices

A. Poor Law Expenditure in various West Riding parishes (£s)

Nov.–Nov.[1]	Emley	Morley	Dewsbury	Alverthorpe	Wakefield
1790-1	101	247	552	496	1,911
1791-2	90	267	449	453	1,786
1792-3	97	377	482	480	1,977
1793-4	136	400	626	636	1,827
1794-5	217	534	836	652	2,545
1795-6	189	601	543	690	2,774
1796-7	243	424	1,088	910	1,801

Easter–Easter[2] Sheffield

1790-1	4,614
1791-2	4,454
1792-3	4,401
1793-4	5,691
1794-5	7,545
1795-6	8,688
1796-7	10,319

B. Production indices

1. Woollen Broad and Narrow cloth milled in West Riding (million yards)[3]

	Broad	Narrow		Broad	Narrow
1790	5·2	4·6	1794	6·1	4·6
1791	5·8	4·8	1795	7·8	5·2
1792	6·8	5·5	1796	7·8	5·2
1793	6·1	4·8	1797	7·1	5·5

2. Cutlery Trades – Wage payments of a large firm in the Sheffield Trade (£s)[4]

1790	549	1794	704
1791	721	1795	708
1792	1,100	1796	966
1793	890	1797	832

3. Silver Trades – Weight of silver marked at Sheffield Assay Office annually (Jan–Jan) (troy pounds)[5]

1790	3,374	1794	2,846
1791	3,137	1795	2,797
1792	3,666	1796	3,339
1793	2,979	1797	2,663

1. Nov.–Nov. figures from Fitzwilliam Papers, Wentworth Woodhouse Muniments, F 47/14, held by Sheffield Central Reference Library. Reproduced by permission of Earl Fitzwilliam and his trustees.
2. *Sheffield Local Register.* Sheffield 1830.
3. A. Gayer, W. Rostow and A. Schwartz, *The Growth and Fluctuation of the British Economy 1790-1850*, Clarendon Press 1953, pp.18, 40.
4. Wage Books of Thomas Nowill and Co., Bradbury Collection, Sheffield Central Reference Library.
5. Figures by permission of the Assay Master, Sheffield Assay Office.

NOTES

1. W. Greenwood, *Memoir of the Life, Ministry and Correspondence of the late George Sykes of Rillington, Malton 1827*, p.55.

2. J. Moon to T. Coke, 22 Aug 1794, letter in *M(ethodist) M(agazine)*, vol. XVIII, London 1795, p.418.

3. E. P. Thompson, *The Making of the English Working Class*, Penguin 1968, p.419.

4. Ibid., p.428.

5. Ibid., pp.428-9.

6. Ibid., p.427.

7. Ibid., p.427.

8. Ibid., p.429.

9. E. J. Hobsbawm, *Primitive Rebels*, Manchester University Press 1959, chapter VIII.

10. E. J. Hobsbawm and G. Rudé, *Captain Swing: the agricultural labourers rising of 1830*, Lawrence & Wishart 1968, pp.288-91.

11. G. Himmelfarb, *Victorian Minds*, Weidenfeld & Nicolson 1968, pp.292-9. While Miss Himmelfarb's interpretation of Thompson and Hobsbawm's failure to confront each other in terms of their conspiring 'to present a common front against a united enemy' appears as the product of an overworked imagination, her regret that such a dialogue has not taken place is justifiable.

12. Thompson, op. cit., pp.917-23.

13. This is the position of one of Thompson's major conservative critics, R. M. Hartwell. In an Addendum to a reprinting of his first attack on Thompson, R. Currie and R. M. Hartwell, 'The Making of the English Working Class?', *Economic History Review*, 2nd series XVIII, no. 3, Dec 1965, which appears in R. M. Hartwell, *The Industrial Revolution and Economic Growth*, Methuen 1971, Hartwell justifies his failure to reply to Thompson's Postscript reply to Currie and Hartwell's original attack by stating '... much of the argument is concerned with irreconcilable differences in political beliefs', pp.375-6.

14. Michael Hill, *A Sociology of Religion*, Heinemann 1973, chapter IX.

15. For a fuller discussion of the problems facing the Methodist polity see J. Walsh, 'Methodism at the end of the Eighteenth Century', *A History of the Methodist Church in Great Britain*, vol. 1 ed. R. Davies and G. Rupp, Epworth Press 1965.

16. J. Sigston, *Life and Ministry of William Bramwell*, 2 vols, London 1872, vol. 1, p.76.

17. V. Ward, *Memoir of the late John Nelson (the second)*, London 1831, p.27.

18. Ibid., pp.27-9.

19. See p.50 and Appendix.

20. Ward, op. cit., p.29.

21. Sigston, op. cit., p.76.

22. Ward, op. cit., p.29.

23. W. Bramwell, *A Short Account of the Life and Death of Ann Cutler*, Sheffield 1796, p.1.

24. Sigston, op. cit., p.86.

25. J. Ward, *Historical Sketches of the Rise and Progress of Methodism in Bingley*, Bingley 1863, p.47.

26. Sigston, op. cit., p.89.

27. See p.50 and Appendix.

28. Ward (V.), op. cit., p.32.

29. Sigston, op. cit., p.83.

30. Ibid., p.87.

31. F. A. West, *Memoir of Jonothan Saville*, London 1857, p.3.

32. J. U. Walker, *A History of Wesleyan Methodism in Halifax and its vicinity*, London 1836, pp.193-6.

33. T. Entwisle, *Memoir of the Reverend Joseph Entwisle*, London 1867, p.112.

34. A. Mather and T. Coke, undated letter in *M.M.* vol. XVII, London 1794, p.603.

35. Ibid., pp.603-6.

36. Bramwell, op. cit., p.2.

37. G. Wood to T. Coke, letter of 7 June 1794, *M.M.* vol. XVIII, London 1795, p.519.

38. Entwisle, op. cit., p.110.

39. Ibid., p.113.

40. Ibid., p.111, my italics.

41. Ibid., p.112.

42. Ibid., pp.111-17.

43. Ibid., p.123.

44. G. Wood to T. Coke, *M.M.* vol. XVIII, p.519.

45. J. Moon to T. Coke, letter of 22 Aug 1794, *M.M.* vol. XVIII, pp.414-15, my italics.

46. W. Bramwell, *Biography of Henry Longden*, Liverpool 1813, p.89.

47. J. Moon to T. Coke, *M.M.* vol. XVIII, p.417.

48. V. Ward, *Memoir of the late Reverend John Nelson*, p.32. Similar recollections of the revival in the West Riding in the summer of 1794 can be found in J. Everett, *The Village Blacksmith or Piety and Usefulness Exemplified in a memoir of the Life of Samuel Hicks, late of Micklefield, Yorkshire*, London 1865, pp.60-4, where the activities of 'Praying George' and 'Praying William', two colliers, humble lay-revivalists like Jonothan Saville, are described.

49. W. Bramwell, *A Short Account of the Life and Death of Ann Cutler*, pp.22-8, where a letter appears dated 3 Nov 1794 written by her from Manchester to a sister in Blackburn which throws much light on the chronology of revival in Lancashire.

50. T. Harrison, *Memoir of the Reverend William Bramwell*, London n.d., p.50. He stated in an undated letter of 1795 to his friend J. Drake, 'I believe God has sent me here, but I cannot tell why, almost every night there is a shaking among the people.'

51. Ibid., p.57.

52. J. Sigston, *Life and Ministry of William Bramwell*, vol. 2, p.29, a letter dated 12 Sept 1796 written from Stavely, Derbyshire.

53. J. G. Rule, 'The Labouring Miner in Cornwall c. 1740-1870', unpublished Warwick University PhD thesis, Warwick 1971.

54. For discussion of 'neuro-physiological' mechanics see W. Sargant, *Battle for the Mind*, Heinemann 1957, who examines the parallels of thought reform, religious revivalism and psychotheraphy, illustrating how

they have in common the generation of excessive cortical excitation producing states of emotional exhaustion and reduced resistance ('hypersuggestibility') in which victims are converted to new points of view. See general discussion in J. A. C. Brown, *Techniques of Persuasion*, Penguin 1971, chapter IX.

55. V. Ward, *Memoir of the late Reverend John Nelson*, p.27.

56. *Letters of John Atlay and John Wesley concerning Dewsbury preaching House*, North Shields 1790, a pamphlet in Dewsbury Public Library.

57. Entwisle, op. cit., p.58.

58. Harrison, op. cit., p.50, an undated letter of 1795 written to J. Drake. The 'miracle' referred to was the regaining of her sight by a woman in the Derbyshire village of Eyam.

59. G. Wood to T. Coke, *M.M.* vol. XVIII, pp.519-20.

60. J. Moon to T. Coke, *M.M.* vol. XVIII, p.417.

61. Walker, op. cit., p.196, a letter of J. Lomas dated 6 June 1794, Entwisle, op. cit., p.111. For a survey of contemporary studies into the association of the periods of childhood and adolescence and religious awareness see M. Argyle, *Religious Behaviour*, Routledge & Kegan Paul 1958, pp.58-65.

62. J. Moon to T. Coke, *M.M.* vol. XVIII, pp.519-20.

63. Sigston, op. cit., vol. 2, p.377, a letter of W. E. Miller of Sheffield to a friend in Manchester, undated, 1796.

64. See Appendix, pp. 70-71.

65. *Sheffield Iris* 27 Feb–13 March 1795 (influenza outbreak-pestilence), *Sheffield Iris* 6 March (famine), *Sheffield Iris* 20 November (earthquake) and *Sheffield Iris* 13 February (flooding).

66. For Brothers' incredible career see C. Roth, *The Nephew of the Almighty*, London 1933. Brothers' prophetic career had begun in 1791 and was largely confined to London. Early in 1795 his 'word' was being transmitted to the provinces by report and press advertisements of his works and testimonials to the authenticity of his prophecies. According to the *Sheffield Iris* of 13 May 1795 he had sent 'tokens' (pieces of bread) to members of the 'lost tribes' in the town. The *Leeds Mercury* of 21 March 1795, noting Brothers' activities, described an imitator at work in the town of Wakefield in the West Riding.

67. See P. Mantoux, *The Industrial Revolution in the Eighteenth Century*, Methuen 1966, pp.265-6, for discussion of the declining position of the small clothier in the early 1790s in the face of the intensified concentration of capital. G. I. H. Lloyd's *The Cutlery Trades*, Longmans 1913, pp.123-6, briefly describes a similar process at work in the cutlery and associated metal trades of South Yorkshire.

68. Analysis of the existing class book material for two of the largest West Riding circuits only mildly suggests this vulnerability:

Sheffield society (from Sheffield Circuit Class Books in Sheffield City Library)

1792	53%	women members
1796	54%	„ „
1799	61%	„ „

Leeds society (from Leeds Circuit Class Books, incomplete, in Sheepscar Public Library, Leeds)

| 1792 | 68% | women members |
| 1797 | 62% | „ „ |

69. G. A. Williams, *Artisans and Sans-Culottes*, Edward Arnold 1968, provides the most concise account drawing on the unpublished theses of Seamen (London University PhD 1954) and Walvin (York University DPhil 1969). I have also found A. V. Mitchell's 'Radicalism and Repression in the North 1791-7' (unpublished Manchester University MA 1958) a valuable source.

70. Thompson, op. cit., pp.427-31.

71. Currie and Hartwell, art. cit., pp.640-1.

72. Thompson, op. cit., p.922.

73. Currie and Hartwell, art. cit., pp.640-1.

74. Material relating to outside West Riding from A. V. Mitchell. West Riding material from my own researches.

75. W. Bramwell, *A Short Account of the Life and Death of Ann Cutler*, op. cit., p.22.

76. P. Stigant, 'Wesleyan Methodism and Working Class Radicalism in the North 1792-1821', *Northern History*, vol. VI, 1971, p.101.

77. Entwisle, op. cit., p.92.

78. J. Musgrove, *The Origins of Methodism in Bolton*, Bolton 1865, p.37.

79. Greenwood, op. cit., p.55. See Isaiah 2.18-21.

80. *Sheffield Register*, 19 November–30 November 1792.

81. Col. De Lancey to Secretary at War, 13 June 1792, H(ome) O(ffice) papers in P(ublic) R(ecord) O(ffice), HO 42/20. The SSCI had claimed in a letter to the London Society of Constitutional Information a 2,400 membership, S. Ashton to J. Adams 26 May 1792, T(reasury) S(olicitor's) papers, TS 11/952/3496, in PRO.

82. *Sheffield Register*, 10 May 1793. The petition was dismissed as 'insolent'.

83. C. Hundley of Leeds Constitutional Society to Society for Constitutional Information, 28 May 1793, John Harrison (of SSCI) in Birmingham on 'missionary' work to SCI 19 March 1793 and in Coventry to SCI, 22 July 1793. All in TS 11/953/3497.

84. *Sheffield Register*, 20 December 1793.

85. *Sheffield Register*, 30 May 1794.

86. Deposition of William Broomhead before the Privy Council, 28 May 1794, TS 11/963/3509. There was a similar shift in the policy of the LCS. See Thompson, op. cit., p.146.

87. *Sheffield Register*, 7 March 1794 (5-6,000 present), *Sheffield Register*, 11 April 1794 (10-12,000 present).

88. Deposition of William Broomhead before the Privy Council, 28 May 1794, TS 11/963/3509, and before Sir Richard Ford, 23 June 1794, TS 11/956/3561.

89. For formation of such corps in the West Riding see *Sheffield Register*, 6 June 1794 and *Leeds Mercury*, 31 May 1794.

90. See 'voices' of George Sykes and John Moon quoted in introduction.

91. *Sheffield Iris*, 7 August 1794.

92. *Sheffield Iris*, 5, 12, 19 and 26 December 1794, records meetings held to celebrate acquittals.

93. Ibid., 14 August, 4 December 1795 reported holding of public meetings. These were curtailed by 36 Geo. III c.8.

94. Entwisle, op. cit., p.125.

95. Paine reading among Methodists is recorded in Walker, op. cit., p.217. Similar activity was recorded by one of John Reeves' correspondents

from the same area, J. Taylor of Horbury to J. Reeves, 2 March 1793, letter-book of the Association for the Protection of Life and Property, British Museum Additional Manuscript Collection 16925.

96. Originals in Sheffield Central Reference Library.

97. Sources for Committee listed:

Beale – TS 11/892/3035.

Broomhead – TS 11/963/3509, TS 11/892/3035.

Grainger – *Sheffield Iris*, 4 July 1794.

Hill – H. Yorke, *The Trial of Henry Redhead Yorke, his own account.* Sheffield 1795, p.149.

Oakes – T. B. Howell, *State Trials*, London 1820, vol. XXV, p.666.

Watson – *Sheffield Iris*, 4 July 1794.

Kent – H. Yorke, op. cit., p.143.

98. Howell, op. cit., pp.663-7.

99. *A Serious Lecture for the Fast Day, Sheffield 1794*, pamphlet in Sheffield Central Library Pamphlets Collection.

100. List of local preachers of the New (Kilhamite) Connexion in the Sheffield circuit in 1797, in Spedding Mss. Collection, vol. V, p.4, Sheffield Central Reference Library.

101. *Sheffield Courant*, 21 December 1793.

102. J. Wilson, *The Songs of Joseph Mather*, Sheffield 1862, pp.vii-x.

103. The Sheffield Kilhamites took over the chapel of an Independent Methodist congregation in Scotland Street which had been ministered to by the Reverend Thomas Bryant, a friend of Kilham's before the secession of 1797 who had acted as an intermediary between the London Corresponding Society and the SSCI in 1792 (letter of T. Hardy, secretary of LCS to T. Bryant, 8 March 1792, British Museum Additional Mss. 27,811. Among the Kilhamites were found members of a new physical force radical party dedicated to revolutionary action who were active both in the Despard business of 1802 and in the attempted rising of 1817. For an attempt to examine the continuities in the revolutionary tradition see J. L. Baxter and F. K. Donnelly, 'Sheffield and the English Revolutionary Tradition 1795-1820' (unpublished paper, Sheffield 1973).

104. Stigant, art. cit., passim.

5 Making Sense and Meaning: A Documentary Method of Analysis

Ross McLeod

Growing dissatisfaction with established research procedures among sociologists of religion has spurred on the search for new methods that hopefully might fall between the two stools of rarefied theoretical generalization and empiricist myopia. Robertson and Campbell,[1] in calling for new research procedures, have suggested two 'orientations' which they feel could yield some fruitful analyses of contemporary religion as it is held, used selectively or rejected by people *in their everyday lives*.

The first 'orientation' prescribes the analysis of 'sites of cultural concern' in which a significant number of people feel that something hitherto taken for granted in British cultural life has become problematic and therefore worthy of great concern and eventual resolution. The second 'orientation' prescribes an 'in-depth analysis' of everyday religiosity in which the sociologist would concern himself with 'the operation of transcendent meaning resources in everyday encounters'.[2] The purpose of this article is to sketch briefly a mode of analysis that seeks to encompass both these 'orientations'.

While the substance of the interview analysed below is thoroughly secular in nature, the problems inherent in such an analysis are highy similar to those incurred by investigators of 'subterranean theology',[3] popular religion or religious sects when studied *from the perspective of the actor in his everyday life*. Some of these problems can be enumerated as follows:
1. How does one determine whether individuals really believe the official beliefs of societies, movements, groups, subgroups and sects of which they appear to be members?
2. If members do really believe the official beliefs, how deeply committed are members to their group or groups?

3. How effective is the group or groups in catering to the needs of members?
4. How does one determine the actual socio-political location of a group as distinct from the location projected in the utopian rhetoric of priests and ideologues?
5. How does one recognize multiple membership, whether the member pays allegiance to two or more distinct groups or holds simultaneous membership in a large group and one of that group's splinter or subgroups?

As ordinary members of society and even as sociologists analysing interviews we are aware that people do not always mean precisely what they say or even say immediately what they mean in reply to questions. Rather, they often use metaphor, double entendres, slogans, innuendo etc., and we almost always have to wait until later in their remarks to feel we have acquired a sufficient *sense* of their replies to be able to know what they really mean. Part of acquiring this *sense* is our almost automatic checking of present statements against previous statements to see if they *hang together*.[4] At the level of normal interaction in everyday life this is the process of *getting to know the other*. For the sociologist seeking to make his methods explicit, repeatable and capable of generalization, this procedure presents a more complex problem.

Following Mannheim and Schutz, Garfinkel and Cicourel discuss some of the 'interpretive procedures' that all actors employ in communicating with each other.[5] The two procedures most central to present purposes are the *retrospective-prospective sense of occurrence* and the *et cetera principle*.[6] The first procedure allows an actor to grasp the sense of an utterance by noting what was said before it and waiting for what will be said after it, thus placing the utterance in the emergent meaning of a conversation. The second procedure allows speakers to leave many things vague or unspoken for the listener to fill in on the assumption that social life operates under standard principles. The two procedures when taken together direct our attention to the documentary method's central dynamic whether used by the actors themselves or by sociologists. This is that individual utterances are not only documentary evidences of an underlying pattern or sense, but also that this underlying sense is required in fully understanding the individual utterances.

When one deals with an incipient social movement that is

developing within and is attempting to broaden a 'site of cultural concern' one finds that Robertson and Campbell's two 'orientations' are two sides of the same coin. A 'site of cultural concern' is at least an indication that a failure of legitimation has taken place and that those segments of everyday life that rely on this legitimation for their meaning have become problematic for the individuals who used to take their meaning for granted. Such a failure in legitimation and the inevitable problems it produces is a familiar dynamic in contemporary society and has been deftly summarized by Martin:

> Once the blanket terminology of legitimation is abandoned one is left either with very high order values of no immediate and obvious application or else the highly unrealistic situational vocabulary of the militant cell ... The difficulty is to locate a critical vocabulary for ongoing political issues of the middle range without being hopelessly compromised in everyday political activity. Eternal verity and political contingency sort ill together.[7]

It is at this level of everyday activity that the second 'orientation' mentioned above poses the question of how individuals create meaning in mundane affairs from meaning resources which in Martin's words are 'very high order values of no immediate and obvious application'. No social movement, group or society can provide anything like a complete set of contingency plans with which members can order the variegated encounters of their everyday lives. They can only provide values, exemplars, testimonials, role models, prophets, priests, confessors, therapeutic agencies[8] and the like, leaving the individual as the final negotiator between the ought and the is of everyday life. Thus it is the individual member we must study if we want to know both the nature of the 'site of cultural concern' and the nature and source of meaning resources as they are used by the member in his everyday life.

One of the more interesting 'sites of cultural concern' in contemporary Britain and elsewhere is the often volatile discussion around the status, role, nature and future of women. This concern has recently generated the Women's Liberation Movement which seeks both answers to the questions that spawned it and a widening and intensification of the site of concern. Having abandoned, or at least rendered traditional legitimations concerning the status of women highly problematic, members find themselves in a very young social movement that has not yet generated much more than slogans calling for general equality with men. Members are thus presented with a rather limited store of alternative meaning resources with which to negotiate meaning in their everyday lives.

Inevitably a 'site of cultural concern' generates ideological statements, manifestoes, creeds, statements of belief and the like. These value or moral statements must, however, be supplemented with viable typologies and strategies based on the higher order values and capable of eventually generating a critical vocabulary for middle range activity as Martin has described. Strategies are methods of maintaining the accent of reality around the beliefs and praxis of the group when confronted with conflicting beliefs and practices. Obviously such strategies for the maintenance of a separate primary reality[9] will be the more crucial as the beliefs and praxis of the group are seen to be deviant by a potentially hostile society.

Ideal types developed or redefined by the group can and often do act singly or in concert (clusters) to defend the particular reality in the group by generating just such a critical vocabulary as Martin has described. New typologies once learned (routinized) to the point of automatically providing categories with which the member may interpret the world, provide an armour of concepts with which the member may manipulate the world around her that often threatens the new reality she has come to accept. Beliefs held hitherto may now be seen as misguided, hostile individuals, institutions and events labelled and devalued and so on.

If one looks at the Women's Liberation Movement one sees several manifestoes almost completely overlapping one another. The manifesto of the Women's Liberation Workshop provides the negatively phrased values below (VN) from which may be derived their positively phrased correlates (V). This document is the most general encompassing statement and has actually been read by the largest number of members.

From this document one can derive a *minimum* list of official values that are presented to members of the movement as alternatives to those actually current in the everyday world. Assent to these general higher order values constitutes minimum requirements for movement membership. Different members, however, will find different values more salient and useful according to their various personal biographies and individual purposes at hand. One index of the success of the movement will be the number of official values members are seen to have actually routinized and the extent to which these are employed in their everyday lives.

Minimum List of Official Values (or Morals)[10]

VN Negatively Stated	V Positively Stated Correlates
1. Women are [generally] oppressed.	1. Women should be at least as free as men.
2. Women are economically oppressed.	2. Women should receive at least as much economic reward as men.
3. Women are commercially exploited by adverts, television and the press.	3. Women should not be more vulnerable than men to such commercial exploitation.
4. Women have an inferior legal status.	4. Women should at least have full legal equality with men.
5. Women are brought up to feel inadequate [inferior] to men.	5. Women should at least be brought up to feel themselves on an equal footing with men.
6. Women receive an inferior education.	6. Women should at least receive an education equal to that of men.
7. Women are brought up and encouraged to compete with and be suspicious of each other in their pursuit of and deferment to men.	7. Women should at least recognize that they face common problems and unite in order to solve them.

Minimum List of Ideal Types (or Categorical Definitions) Officially Available[11]

T1. Sexism – course of action type[12]

Sexist – personal ideal type

T2. Male chauvinism – course of action type
Male chauvinist – personal ideal type

T3. Consciousness raising – course of action type
Aware person – personal ideal type

T4. Sisterhood – course of action type
Sister – personal ideal type

T5. Liberation – course of action type
Liberated – personal ideal type

Minimum List of Official Strategies for Maintaining a Feminist Reality

S1. The development of awareness from one's individual problems, anxieties etc., to their existence in similar form amongst large numbers of women, to their eventual source in society, i.e. consciousness raising.

S2. The analysis of one's situation *qua* woman starts from one's own personal feelings, i.e. the politics of experience.

S3. No purely individual solutions to the problems of women are, in the long term, possible.

Having derived sets of minimum values, types and strategies from the movement's literature one then determines whether these particulars are actually used. To what extent they are used can be judged by a close reading of lengthy, open-ended, tape-recorded interviews with members of the movement. What follows is an elaboration of this procedure with just one interview that runs to well over ten thousand words in typescript. While the analysis of the respondent's conversation is not exhaustive it is highly representative of those sections not included. The particulars occurring that the respondent has generated herself will have a higher number than the official particulars, e.g. V8-Vn, T6-Tn, S4-Sn.

Particulars are most often found in clusters and official particulars are no exception. Note above that S1 and T3 are associated inasmuch as S1 is a strategy for helping to produce and maintain a feminist reality and T3 is the praxis it produces in the everyday world. In a similar way V7 is associated with T4 and VN7, of which V7 is the positively phrased correlate. The interassociations of these five particulars can be represented as follows and may be called the original cluster.

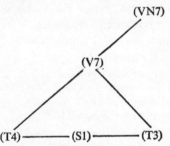

Q. Why did you continue [Women's Lib.] meetings if you found the first one rather intimidating?

A.1.0. '... I was attracted by the chance of meeting other people. I didn't have any friends' (particular=S4).

Comment W.L. does not self consciously recruit the socially isolated. In this case of a member who explicitly describes herself as having been friendless we can log the offer of a group of potential friends as an unofficial personal strategy (conscious or otherwise) for the maintenance of a feminist reality.

A.1.1. '... I saw a lot of people there [in W.L. group] who were not content with the way things were and when I put forward my theories why I was content – they questioned and while I defended them at the time – it was a sort of impetus to go back and ask why they should think so differently to me and to find out more about the sort of thing they said' (S3).

Q. Do you think Women's Lib. has lived up to any of the expectations you may have brought to it?
A.2.0. '... whatever has happened has happened as I became more aware of things ... recently I have been wondering why I am in the movement and what good is has done for me. I can see that it has made me a lot more aware of a lot of things. That hasn't necessarily made me a lot happier' (T3 in original cluster).

Q. Do you think you have changed in any way since joining the movement?
A.3.0. 'Yes, I think I value my own thoughts and feelings far more than I ever did' (S2).
A.3.1. 'I used to think that a lot of my feelings were just pure imagination or imaginary thought peculiar to me and nobody else' (T3 in original cluster).

Q. What were these feelings?
A.4.0. 'Feelings like, how could I be satisfied by spending all my time with children. It didn't seem to be particularly fulfilling, although I was told ... I had the idea it was supposed to be ...' (T6).
Comment The respondent, while alluding to the familiar ideal type of the fulfilled mother, indicates that she holds a negative version of this type. Such outlines of a type generated from the respondent's personal biography may be logged as T6 and clarification awaited.
A.4.1. '... feelings of inadequacy and lack of confidence about how other people regarded me ...' (VN5-V5 implicit).
A.4.2. '... and just feelings about other people that I might express, but not having the confidence to say that if I think it – it is valid' (VN5-V5 implicit).

Q. Any other ways in which you have changed?
A.5.0. 'My attitude towards other women, my attitudes to marriage. I think before Women's Lib., there was always a feeling of competitiveness with other women because I used to meet them

with other men and even if I wasn't in outright competition, like trying to gain the attention of one particular man, there was always this thing ...' (VN7 in original cluster).

A.5.1. 'I really feel a difference between spending time with women as compared to spending time with men and women of men ...' (VN7, T4 in original cluster).

Q. What about relationships with men? Have they changed since you joined Women's Lib.?

A.6.0. 'I don't feel so intimidated by men ...' (VN5-V5 implicit).

A.6.1. 'Now my attitudes have changed a lot. I am much more critical of them, obviously' (T2).

Q. So you eventually got things [the problem of dependency] sorted out with your husband in that respect?

A.7.0. 'In a way, because I felt that I could just see us ending like my mum and dad. My mother is completely dependent on my father. My father feels that he has never explored his own potential as a person, and I didn't want my husband to be like that. I didn't want me to be like that ...' (T7).

Q. Do you think that this event with your husband [his affair with a mutual woman friend, at first condoned by respondent] has done anything for you? Can you think of any other things which might have changed since?

A.8.0. 'I am very much more aware of his chauvinism. I am much more aware of what he is out to get ...' (T2).

A.8.1. 'I am beginning to realize the things that bothered me before – but I just thought well that's me – I am just funny or just wrong or something. I now realize the specific male traits for what they are' (T2, T3, S2 in elaborated cluster below).

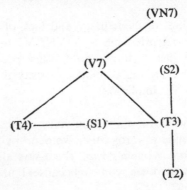

Particular	T3	S1	VN7	T4	V7	T2	VN5	V5	S3	S2	S4	T6	T7	S5	T8
1. Explicit occurrences	4	2	2	1	0	3	3	0	1	3	2	1	1	1	1
2. Implicit occurrences, i.e. in a cluster of two or more particulars	4	6	6	7	8	3	0	3	0	2	0	0	0	0	0
3. % explicit occurrences in total occurrences	50	25	25	13	0	50	100	0	100	60	100	100	100	100	100
4. % implicit occurrences in total occurrences	50	75	75	88	100	50	0	100	0	40	0	0	0	0	0
5. % explicit occurrences to total explicit occurrences	16	8	8	4	0	12	12	0	4	12	8	4	4	4	4
6. % implicit occurrences to total implicit occurrences	10	15	15	18	20	8	0	8	0	5	0	0	0	0	0
7. % of explicit plus implicit occurrences to total of all occurrences both explicit and implicit	12	12	12	12	12	9	5	5	8	8	3	2	2	2	2

Q. Can you think back to what you were like before [you joined W.L.] in personal terms and in achievement terms?

A.9.0. 'In personal terms I was unaware of myself and other people' (T3 in elaborated cluster).

Q. You say that you have ideals but you find it difficult to work them out in practical life.

A.10.0. 'I have realized that the concept and the emotional response were completely different things, and made me examine again ... how much our upbringing and conditioning has a hold on us. So you could have great fantasies about how things could be but also realize that what you are working on, which is yourself, is the product of a certain conditioning and a certain way of life' (S1, S2 in elaborated cluster).

Q. Do you ever try to get the women in your play group to come to the meetings?

A.11.0. 'No, I don't specifically. I talk to them about things, but I don't ask them to come. I am very wary about that because I think women are wary about Women's Lib., and I feel it might break my contact with them if I asked them to come because they might feel that whatever I said would be with this idea in my mind, and so they might become very suspicious. I do talk about things and if a topic comes up I give my ideas quite freely, but I don't ask them to come' (T8, S5).

Comment T8 is the type covering the respondent's statement that non-W.L. members are 'suspicious' or 'wary' of the movement. S5 is the strategy that follows from T8, viz., proselytization in a low key only.

Q. What aspects of the group [the local W.L. group] do you find you enjoy?

A.12.0. 'I think I like seeing the people in the group. It is nice to hear about other experiences, because it makes you realize you are not the only one with these feelings' (S1, S4 in further elaborated cluster below).

On page 85 are listed the occurrences of particulars both explicitly and also as members of clusters. Occurrences are generative in the sense that once a particular becomes an explicit member of a cluster then it will carry on as an implicit member of that

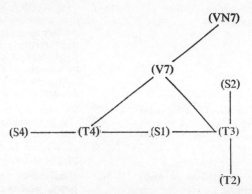

cluster until such time as a contradiction arises. Only a contradiction that is recognized as being so by the actor is strictly speaking a contradiction.

For the relatively taken for granted particulars one looks for high percentages reading along columns 4 and 6, while the relatively problematic is indicated by high percentages in column 5. Thus in descending order of intensity we have the situation sketched below.

Relatively Taken for Granted		Relatively Problematic	
1. (V7)	Women should at least recognize that they face common problems and unite in order to solve them.	1. (T3)	Consciousness raising or aware person.
2. (T4)	Sisterhood or sister.	2. (T2)	Male chauvinism or male chauvinist.
3. (S1)	The development of awareness from one's individual problems, anxieties etc., to their existence in similar form against large numbers of women, to their eventual source in society, i.e. consciousness raising.	3. (S2)	The analysis of one's situation *qua* woman starts from one's own personal feelings, i.e. the politics of experience.
4. (VN5)	Women are brought up to and encouraged to compete with and be suspicious of each other in their pursuit of and deferment to men.	4. (VN5)	Women are brought up to feel inadequate [inferior to men].

5. (T3) Consciousness raising or   5. (S1) The development of aware-
         aware person.   ness from one's individual
                                               problems, anxieties etc., to
                                               their existence in similar
                                               form amongst large numbers
                                               of women, to their eventual
                                               source in society, i.e. con-
                                               sciousness raising.

6. (V5) Women should at least be   6. (VN7) Women are brought up
         brought up to feel them-   and encouraged to compete
         selves on an equal footing   with and be suspicious of
         with men.   each other in their pursuit
                                               of and deferment to men.

7. (T2) Male chauvinism or male   7. (S4) Opportunity of meeting
         chauvinist.   people and making friends.

As might be expected with a first-year member in a very young social movement, the relatively problematic tends to overshadow the relatively taken for granted. The explanation for this lies both with the member and with the movement.

A very young social movement that has not had sufficient time to generate a range of types and strategies of adequate depth and sophistication runs the risk of forcing its members into a Manichean militancy when confronted with opposition from the everyday world. Thus with our respondent above the fundamental strategy (S1) is taken for granted yet very occasionally becomes problematic. A check back shows that in the two explicit occurrences of (S1) the respondent realized the centrality of consciousness raising to the maintenance of the reality of feminist values. The praxis and characteriological type (T3) associated with (S1) while being a little less taken for granted is also highly problematic. This is because while the course of action type (T3) is both well defined and a crucial element of movement membership the personal ideal type (T3) is still either vague or often a question of considerable debate. Without a highly developed analysis available to members they must frequently revert to (T3) when explaining how they came to their present position and what that position is.

On the other hand (T2)'s appearance as both relatively taken for granted and also as highly problematic reflects the personal position of the member. A check back to the explicit occurrences of (T2) shows that the respondent frequently invokes this ideal type in understanding her husband. Again the lack of refinement or discrimination in the available types leaves the member little choice in the labels she applies. One can legitimately speak of the degree of manipulation of the environment possible by an actor using the types and strategies available. The cruder the types or categorical definitions the more heavily the member must rely on strategies to maintain their reality in the face of contrary information.

Drawing on the documentary method of analysis sketched above answers can be suggested for the five questions posed at the beginning of this essay.

1. To determine whether individuals really believe the official beliefs of societies, groups or sects one must discover whether the official beliefs in question act as significant meaning resources in their everyday lives. Through the documentary method of analysis here proposed one can build up an adequate picture of members' meaning resources through the values, types and strategies they employ. If very few or none of the meaning resources offered by the group in question are employed as taken for granted resources by the actor then one may conclude that they are not in fact believed.

2. To determine the degree of commitment of an actor to the beliefs of the group one must – following the procedures sketch above – examine which elements of the available meaning resources are taken for granted in the actor's negotiation of everyday encounters and the depth to which these meaning resources have been routinized.

3. In determining the effectiveness of the group in catering to member's needs one must answer two questions from data similar to that generated by the documentary method of analysis sketched above. Firstly, which official particulars are problematic for members and why are they so? Secondly, which particulars has the member had to generate herself and why has she had to do so?

4. In distinguishing the actual socio-political location of a group from the impressions conveyed by the rhetoric of the group's officials one must have recourse to members' actual accounts.[13] When accounts are analysed as those above one can compute the frequency of particulars taken for granted, problematic particulars and those ignored by members. In this way a picture of a group's real location is obtained.

5. Using the documentary method of analysis to analyse a large

number of interviews or participant observation data, one can generate *real* vocabularies of group membership. As was seen above such vocabularies (collections of particulars) can be charted in depth (intensity) as well as in breadth. Interest, splinter, ginger or subgroups will develop their own defining particulars (subvocabularies) which can be carefully noted and used to gauge a member's drift within the larger group as she begins to routinize particulars that are tied to one subgroup, wing or lobby.

NOTES

1. Roland Robertson and Colin Campbell, 'Religion in Britain: the Need for New Research Strategies', *Social Compass* XIX, 1972, p.185.

2. Ibid., p.194.

3. David Martin, *A Sociology of English Religion*, SCM Press and Heinemann 1967, p.74.

4. Only those carefully schooled in seeing *nonsense* in the layman's everyday pragmatism – ideologues, judges, some professional sociologists, priests etc. – and *sense* of coherency in interaction will yearn for a systematic consistency that actors rarely exhibit.

5. Harold Garfinkel, *Studies in Ethnomethodology*, Prentice-Hall, NJ 1967, pp.39-42 and ch. 3; Aaron V. Cicourel, *Cognitive Sociology*, Penguin 1973, pp.84-8; cf. Peter McHugh, *Defining the Situation*, Bobbs-Merrill, NY 1968.

6. Cicourel, ibid., his italics.

7. David Martin, 'An Essay in Conceptual and Empirical Synthesis', *Acts of the 12th International Conference on Sociology of Religion (C.I.S.R.)*, Edition du Secrétariat C.I.S.R., 39 Rue de la Monnaie – 59042 Lille (Cédex), France 1973, p.523.

8. For an essay that shares and takes as its subject the theoretical framework behind the analysis presented here see G. N. Howe, 'Pragmatism, Phenomenology and the Strategies of Everyday Life', mimeo, The London School of Economics and Political Science.

9. Cf. situated moral and social orders in *Deviance and Respectability*, ed. Jack Douglas, Basic Books, NY 1970.

10. See *Introduction to the Women's Liberation Workshop*, published from 22 Great Windmill St, London W1.

11. On strategies and types see, for instance, *Sisterhood is Powerful*, ed. Robin Morgan, Vintage Books, NY 1970.

12. For Schutz's distinction between course of action types and personal ideal types see Alfred Schutz, *The Phenomenology of the Social World*, Heinemann Educational Books 1972, pp.186-194.

13. See accounts and accounting procedures in Harold Garfinkel, op. cit., ch. 1.

6 Social Change and the Church of Scotland

Madeleine Maxwell-Arnot

Many features of contemporary religious organizations can best be understood when the church is viewed as a social institution. This is not to deny the importance of the essentially spiritual activities of these institutions, but rather to recognize that a church exists in interaction with a social surround. The Church of Scotland is here examined as a case study in institutional adaptation. The view is presented that the church, like any institution, is constantly undergoing a process of adaptation to environmental changes. In the case of a religious institution adapting to an increasingly secular society, the need for change has become acute. The problem is no longer one of expansion or even stability – it is the need for self-preservation.

As measured by a number of indicators the Church of Scotland is in decline. In 1901, the total church membership[1] quoted in official statistics[2] consisted of 1,163,594 in a population of 4,472,103. In the years between 1960 and 1970 membership fell by 141,465 to 1,154,211 in a population of 5,199,000. The ratio, therefore, of church membership to the Scottish population fell from 1:4 to 1:5 over the 70 years.

Finance too has become a major problem for the church. By 1970 the average donated a year by a church member amounted to £6·19, a rise of some £5 per capita over the last forty years. The Yearbook of the Church of Scotland reports, however, that 'While the index of liberality (givings) per member has risen over the past few years, it has not done so at a rate commensurate with the rise in the index of weekly earnings.'[3]

If one looks at the official statistics for the last 25 years, the general decline of the church is clearly visible (see Table 1 over). The number of working charges is greatly reduced with many still vacant, the number of students completing the course for entry to the ministry in any given year has fallen at the same time as the total number of ministers has dropped. The average number of candidates for the ministry over the past ten years has been 64, where at least 100 are required to make good the wastage caused by deaths and retirements.

TABLE 1

The Church of Scotland (1945-1970)

Year	No. of charges	No. of vacant charges	No. of students completing the course	No. of ministers	No. of chaplains
1945	2,426	161	44	2,265	286
1947	2,837	144	52	2,242	61
1950	2,348	142	99	2,206	44
1952	2,322	140	68	2,182	47
1955	2,289	176	35	2,113	50
1957	2,272	167	59	2,042	41
1960	2,130	171	60	1,959	33
1962	2,069	142	50	1,927	37
1965	2,016	131	50	1,885	36
1967	1,969	155	57	1,814	31
1970	1,902	148	46	1,814	31

Sources: Reports from the General Assembly for the Church of Scotland (1945-70)

Organizational changes in the church can be traced over the last hundred years which appear in an adaptive light, though not always a result of deliberate decision. Prominent among these changes are the increased centralization of financial and administrative government of the church and the growth of an articulated committee network. The church has evolved a structure, the product both of collective effort and emergency measures, that would be unrecognizable a hundred years ago. As one Presbytery clerk exclaimed:

Most of the time of the present day Assembly is occupied with matters of administration. Standing committees – of which there are about thirty –

submit reports of their diligence during the past year and seek approval of their policies for the future. When we remember that the Book of Assembly reports runs to some 800 pages at fully 500 words a page, we get an impression of the amount of administration involved ... we see how completely the Assembly is coming to be an organ of administration. A Rip Van Winkle of a commissioner awakening in a modern Assembly would be much mystified by this. He has no need to be worried for this is how a living Church accommodates itself to a changing situation and if today sees less litigation and more administration who is to say this is a bad thing.[4]

However, the focus of this study is not upon the organizational adaptation at this level but rather on the role of the minister as a key mediator of adaptation of the total institution. It is the minister, above all, who is responsible for keeping the parishes active, for retaining and increasing the congregations and conserving their level of commitment to the church. The minister is the backbone of the church, its symbolic representative as well as its administrator. No amount of organizational change, therefore, can escape the fact that without a sufficient number of ministers, the church is paralysed.

It is becoming increasingly important, therefore, for the church to examine the effects of her recruitment policy in an age when demand for ministers is far greater than supply. It is for this reason that two major questions are concentrated on in this study. First, are the ministers drawn from a cross section of the population or are they recruited selectively? Secondly, how much has recruitment and training policy changed over the last fifty years? It will be shown that not only have geographic catchment areas changed within this century but that the social and educational background of the minister in 1950 is very different from that of the 1910 minister. No longer does the church recruit mainly from the Highlands and rural areas, and no longer do the majority of ministers come from the private school sector. It will also be shown how, by modifying educational entry requirements, there has been a significant change in the type of minister recruited.

It is not sufficient, however, to see such changes in recruitment policy and type of minister selected purely in terms of their effect on the numbers recruited. Such changes have implications for the wide variety of problems previously mentioned for they may well accentuate rather than alleviate a crisis. For example, the increased recruitment of older candidates will result in a shortening of the average career length, and earlier retirement. Greater difficulty will arise later in terms of replacing an ageing ministry than was experienced in recruiting the normal quota needed for replacement. So too will the increased selection of urban ministers affect the problem of filling vacant rural charges for it would not be surprising if they were unwilling to settle in a quiet and isolated parish, having been brought up in the cities.

The conclusions are, of necessity, speculative in that more research is needed. It is imperative, though, that the church must recognize the true effects of changed recruitment policy and patterns if it is to adapt successfully to maintain its position. The first section of this paper, then, examines the historical context of recruitment to the ministry in terms not only of who was considered suitable for the task but also what was understood to be the role of the minister. Recruitment patterns are then examined in terms of the geographic origins, and the social and educational background of the ministers between 1910 and 1950. Training is also studied in the final section, showing the changed recruitment policy in terms of educational requirements for entry to the ministry.

The Traditional Minister

A hundred years ago the ministry was seen as one of the highest professions one could choose. It was said that parents could think of no greater profession for their sons than the ministry. It was respected for being a 'pillar of moral rectitude and sober dignity'.[5] The necessary qualifications for entry into the church were unique; they involved among others 'a consecrated spirit, a well-trained and well-informed mind, and, that somewhat rare and incommunicable gift, sympathy'.[6] The task was seen as vital, the career ennobling. The church was characterized by the qualities of its members, for it had 'the pick of the bright, well disposed young men of all classes',[7] university educated and respectable. Ministers were revered for their learning, their scholarly ability and dedication. A high standard was set for selection, rigorous rules laid down for appropriate behaviour. As Adam Smith, the economist, wrote:

> We readily feel, therefore, that independent of custom, there is a propriety in the manners which custom has allotted to this profession, and that nothing can be more suitable to the character of the clergyman

than that grave, that austere and abstracted severity which we are habituated to expect in his behaviour.[8]

A definition of what the role of being a minister involved in the Church of Scotland may be seen in Knox's[9] explanation of the derivation of the word 'minister'. He claimed it originated from the Greek word 'diakonia' meaning service, denoting not a status but a function. 'The minister is useful to the Church, serving all its members in all possible ways and contributing to the growth and effective functioning of the Church itself.'[10] He quotes Mark (10.43-44) who wrote 'Whoever would be great among you, must be your servant, and whoever would be first among you, must be slave to all'.[11] It is this that distinguishes the ministry from the laity in the Church of Scotland, for where all members have a 'call' to further Christian work, it is only the minister who is called to serve God and the community. Ministers then have no sacred rights, no unique knowledge, only the calling to serve. Their authority, unlike that of the priest in the Roman Catholic Church, is not charismatic – it is legitimated by virtue of their office rather than their sacerdotal qualities. Emphasis, therefore, is placed on enthusiasm and dedication, a capacity for sustained study, the power to arouse interest and enthusiasm in others, the abilities to organize and administer. The personal attributes required are many, the commitment needed is all-encompassing if the minister is to make anything of the office. However, as the Book of Discipline[12] points out 'God hath determined that his church here on earth shall not be taught by angels but by men'.[13]

How then were ministers selected? Who could be considered sufficient to become a minister, for not every man is suitable? It is better, the Book of Discipline says, to have no minister at all, than one who cannot be deemed fit. Even if there is a 'raritie of godlie and learned men', the lack of such able men 'sall nott excuse us befoir God, gif by oure consent unable men be placed over the floken of Christ Jesus'.[14] Not only must they be judged by means of examination 'strait and scharpe' but must be seen to be someone in whose mouth God has put a 'sermon of exhortation'. Recruitment must be based on additional criteria to those of self-selection and occupational choice, more than social skills or personality. What is involved is the notion of a 'divine call' for without a call no one is allowed or ought to take upon himself the office of minister.

According to the church there are two elements in the call to the ministry. There must be the inner calling from God to induce a man to offer himself in service to the church and the outer calling whereby the church asks for his service. The inner calling can come in a variety of ways – it may appear as a sudden compulsion, a conviction that the ministry is the only possible choice; or as a result of a gradual realization of personal and social needs, culminating in a belief in the relevance of the ministry.

The requirement of the call, however, does not mean the standardization of ministers. Each minister has very different expectations and images of the role of the minister and the church. In the past ministers have ranged from 'fiery narrow convenanting field preachers' to 'sanctimonious dissenters'. There have been 'scholars who are invisible six days a week and incomprehensible on Sunday, mild eccentrics, parish tyrants, the indolent and the sottish'.[15] Today one can find evangelists, radicals, conservative pastors and efficient committee men. There are those who see themselves as social workers, and others who devote themselves to scholarly works or histories of their charges. But all have been selected, all are the product of particular recruitment and training policies, whether deliberate or unconscious, and it is to these policies and their effects that we now turn.

Recruitment Trends

1. *Geographic origins*

According to David Moberg[16] in his book *The Church as a Social Institution*, the protestant clergy in America come largely from rural communities. Certainly in 1910, some 47% of the new ministers of the Church of Scotland were from the Highlands, an area mainly rural in character. This proportion, however, began to decrease over the next fifty years so that by 1930 only 28·6% of the recruits were originally highlander, and in 1950 only 21·1% recruited came from the north. The Lowlands, on the other hand, were contributing an increasingly large proportion to the ministerial intake. By 1950, 77·2% of the recruits originated from the Lowland belt in comparison with some 47% in 1910. The Borders never accounted for more than 11·4% (1930) of the new recruits.

There is always a danger, as Moberg points out, of overstressing the role played by rural areas as suppliers of the ministry since the proportion recruited tend to reflect the ecological distribution of the population. It is necessary, therefore, to see if population migration trends can go some way in accounting for the change of recruitment area (see Figure 1 below). Certainly in terms of general direction, the migration trends of the population[17] are directly reflected in the changing recruitment patterns of the ministry. Where the population has left the villages and agricultural areas of the Highlands to flood the Lowland belt, so the proportion of ministers recruited from the south is increased and the highland quota is lowered.

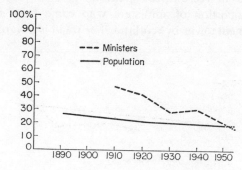

Figure 1(a)   Percentage of Highlanders

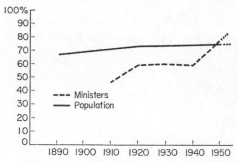

Figure 1(b)   Percentage of Lowlanders

However, it is noticeable that the proportion recruited from the Highlands has been consistently larger than the proportion of the general population living in this area, though the difference between the two is decreasing rapidly. In 1920 some 21·4% of the population contributed 41% of the ministerial recruits. However by 1950 the proportions of the population and the ministry from the Highlands were almost equal. The Lowlands, though, are permanently underrepresented, with a relatively small proportion of ministers being recruited. Whereas in 1920 there were 18% more Lowland than Highland ministers, by 1950 the percentage difference had increased to 56·1%. The major catchment area then for ministerial recruitment appears to have shifted from the Highlands at the turn of the century to the Lowland belt by the mid-century. There is still, however, a slight bias towards the Highland area that cannot be explained by the population statistics.

The change in recruitment patterns is also reflected in the decreasing proportion of ministers who came from rural backgrounds and small towns in Scotland. The trend is towards increased

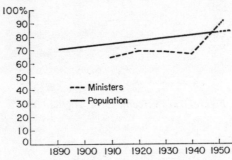

Figure 2(a)   Percentage from Urban Areas

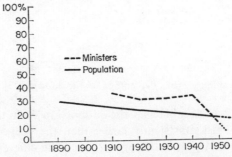

Figure 2(b)   Percentage from Rural Areas

recruitment from the southern belt where the cities and large towns have attracted the population. Sixty years ago the proportion recruited from the villages and agricultural areas consisted of some 35%. By 1950, however, it had dropped to 12%. Small towns and large boroughs during these forty years have contributed on average a third of the total recruitment. The proportion of city ministers has increased over the period from some 29% in 1910 to almost half of all ministers recruited in 1950.

If one compares the census figures for population with the ministerial recruitment statistics (see Figure 2), one can see that part of this trend is explicable by population movement.[18] However it cannot explain why in the first two decades the rural areas supplied more than their share of men. In 1920 the 22·7% of the population living in rural areas accounted for 30·8% of the ministerial recruitment.

However, where the rural population is in general overrepresented, the urban population is underrepresented. In 1910 the ratio of urban to rural ministers was 2 : 1. By 1950, though, the trend seems to have reversed direction and there are seven urban ministers to one rural, a ratio greater in fact than that for the population as a whole (5 : 1). Thus the trend is now towards overrepresentation of urban rather than rural populations.

To conclude, the geographic origins of the ministers appears to have changed, not so much in bias relative to the population, but in terms of the proportions recruited from the Highlands and the Lowlands, from the rural and city areas. There would appear to be a tendency in the past for the Highland and rural areas to provide more than their normal quota of ministers, and the Lowlands and urban areas, though now providing an increasingly greater proportion of the recruitment numbers, to be underrepresented. However, the direction has changed and rural areas would seem to be in danger of filling the place of cities – that of being underrepresented.

2. *Social and educational background*

It is well known that family influences often affect the vocational choice of the ministry. As Moberg[19] points out, ministers' homes have provided as much as 25 times their natural quota of clergymen. In the case of the Church of Scotland, the percentage of ministers in 1910 whose fathers were themselves in the church was unusually high – for exactly one-third of all those recruited were sons of ministers. Even in 1920 the percentage was still very high (22%) but over the period the proportion has dropped steadily until in 1950 there were only 3 out of 70 recruits who had fathers in the church. Self-recruitment, it would seem, is a declining trend.

To turn now to education – it is interesting to compare the Church of Scotland with the Church of England,[20] for where selection procedures were found to be biased, unconsciously if not consciously, towards public and grammar schools and Oxford and Cambridge in the latter church, statistics for recruitment to the Church of Scotland show a completely different trend. Where recruitment from public schools and feepaying schools[21] is concerned, over the 50-year period the percentage of recruits from these schools has dropped from 53·4% in 1910 to 45·5% in 1930 and 15·7% in 1950, with more recruits traditionally selected from the feepaying schools, rather than the few public schools in Scotland. The cut back of the proportion from the feepaying schools is complemented by an increase since 1910 of the proportion from secondary schools and primary schools.

TABLE 2

Type of School Attended

Year	Secondary/ Primary %	Feepaying/ Public %
1910	46·6	53·4
1920	65·8	34·2
1930	54·5	45·5
1940	77·4	22·6
1950	84·3	15·7
Total sample	70·6	29·4

The bias in favour of secondary schools is not surprising if one remembers the number of such schools in Scotland and the paucity of public schools. Feepaying schools have tended to close down from lack of funds or become incorporated into state schools. It also became easier for students in secondary schools to enter university, to obtain funds and to be selected for the church by way of its modified courses and reduced educational requirements.

If one looks at the recruitment patterns in terms of school leaving age, one can see a marked downward trend between 1910 and 1950. The majority of candidates for the ministry in 1910 were 19 years or more when they left school. By mid-century, however, the ministry were recruiting a sizeable proportion of candidates who left school before or at 16 years old.

TABLE 3

School Leaving Age

Year	16 and under %	17 and 18 year olds %	19 and over %
1910	2·6	21·1	76·3
1920	9·0	36·5	54·5
1930	17·8	24·4	57·8
1940	20·0	40·0	40·0
1950	36·7	32·9	30·4
Total sample 20·2		32·8	47·0

This trend of reduced school leaving age may well be a result of the recruitment of those who did not attend university directly after school but went into other occupations as apprentices and trainees. In 1910, 28·1% of the recruits delayed going to university, while in 1930 the proportion reached 36·8%. Over the period, delayed entry on average made up for some 30% of the recruits with the other 70% entering university straight after finishing school.

However, more important than these figures for delayed entrance to university are the statistics for what Coxon[22] called the 'normal' and 'late' entrants. A 'normal' entrant would be the ordinand who came straight from school or university and went into the divinity college, the ministry being his first choice of occupation. The 'late' entrant, on the other hand, would be recruits trained in other occupations before entering the ministry. They could be retired colonels, active professionals such as doctors, lawyers or business-men who decided later in life to enter the ministry. These two types, Coxon found, held very different educational qualifications, came from different backgrounds and entered at different ages.

They appeared to be two discrete populations within the ministerial ranks in the Church of England.

In most of the cohorts sampled in the Church of Scotland, the normal entrants accounted for a greater proportion of ordinands than late entrants (in 1910 and 1930 normal entrants consisted of 54% and 62% respectively with 45·7% and 36·5% late entrants). However, in the years after each of the two World Wars the proportion of late entrants[23] not surprisingly rose. In 1920 there were 51·2% late entrants to 48·8% normal, while in 1950 there were 74·6% late entrants to 25·4% normal entrants.

In terms of their backgrounds, the normal and late entrants in the Church of Scotland seem little different. They appear to be selected in equal proportions from Highland and Lowland towns and villages. There is also no significant difference between the proportion of entrants, whether normal or late, whose fathers were in the church. However, the late entrants do have a consistently higher proportion selected from secondary schools and consistently lower proportion from the feepaying and public schools.

TABLE 4

School Type Attended by Normal and Late Entrants

Year	Entry	Secondary/ Primary %	Feepaying/ Public %
1910	normal	38·9	61·1
	late	54·5	45·5
1920	normal	68·4	31·6
	late	68·4	31·6
1930	normal	47·4	52·6
	late	69·2	30·8
1940	normal	74·5	26·6
	late	81·8	18·2
1950	normal	77·8	22·2
	late	86·6	13·4

Moreover, there is a definite difference in the school-leaving age of each group. In 1910, 87·5% of the late entrants left school after 19 years old compared with 63·2% of the normal entrants. This trend changed, however, so that by 1930 only 40% of the late entrants stayed on at school until 19 years old compared with 71% of the normal entrants. The proportion of late entrants who left school before 16 years old in 1950 had risen to 50·9% whilst only 11·1% of the normal entrants left so young. This relation between young school-leavers and late entrants may well explain the drop in school-leaving age over the period for as more late entrants are recruited so are the younger school-leavers.

Among the qualities required for the ministry, marriage certainly seems to be one, for the ratio of married to unmarried ministers is high. In 1950, the ratio reached 22:1. Few remain unmarried (in 1950 only 4·3% were unmarried) and even fewer marry twice.[24] The proportion who marry daughters of ministers remains very low, never accounting for more than 13·3%, only 4 out of 30 recruits (1910). This is surprising, since daughters of ministers would seem to be most fitting wives for ordinands, having had the experience already of working within a parish.

The normal entrant seems to have married within the first year of his charge, while the late entrant in general seems to have been married before ordination. The higher the proportion of late entrants then, the more likely the recruits will be married before ordination. Some will even have had their first child before induction to their first charge (in 1950 47·3% had their first child before induction). However, these will most probably be late entrants as they are older than normal entrants and are more likely to be family men before entering the ministry.

The type of ministerial recruit, then, has changed, not only in terms of geographic origin but also of social background, and directly related to this change in the type recruited is the modification of entry requirements. It is only by changing the educational qualification needed that the new and different type of minister could be accepted.

Training

The Church of Scotland has always cherished the idea of an educated ministry. However, as Henderson points out, the ideal was not a bookworm. He says: 'To be fit for his position a minister must have at least enough knowledge to recognize his own limitations and should be sufficiently well grounded generally to inspire confidence.'[25] The training was hard and demanding, lasting on average for six to seven years. Students of the highest academic ability were chosen, generally having already completed a first degree at one of the Scottish universities. They were then required to complete a further three years for a Bachelors degree in Theology (B.D.) before being considered a fit candidate for the profession. The course, laid down in the Union of 1929, consisted of the study of the Old and New Testaments, Church History, Systematic and Practical Theology.

The requirement of a university degree, however, has been adapted over the past fifty years and a new modified curriculum has been set up. Those over 25 years old (later 23) were able to study for four years leading to a B.D. degree as a first degree, followed by two years of further study. This meant that candidates did not have to take the initial arts degree.[26] By 1960 applicants were able to enter training for the ministry with only two 'highers' and one Ordinary level pass at school, taking a pre-divinity course and then the modified curriculum that other non-graduates took. Though the limit of the age of entry was placed at 45 years more men over and under that age were able to enter the colleges by taking the modified course if they had professional qualifications that exempted them from the necessity of the arts degree. It also became possible to be recruited without any qualifications, if old enough. Thus over the period a new type of recruit was selected. Older men became more common; the proportion of recruits ordained between the ages of 35 and 45 years rose from 11·4% in 1910 to 13·5% in 1940 and 25·4% in 1950. The younger age group (20 to 35 years), accounting for some 88% in 1910, only accounted for 70·4% in 1950. However, what had far greater implications for the ministry was the increasing proportion of non-graduates.

In the years between 1910 and 1940 only a small proportion of recruits entered with only a B.D. degree where some 70%-80% held Masters degrees as well as the compulsory B.D. degree. However, by 1950, with the opening up of the university system when financial aid became easier to obtain and the educational requirements were dropped, some 43·7% took advantage of the open door to the ministry and only took the B.D. degree. The graduates of the universities now had other occupations and professions open to them, often with a higher status than the ministry, and a smaller and smaller proportion of the recruits entered with a first degree.

When one looks at the degree level of the normal and late entrants in 1950, one can understand such a drastic drop in the educational level of the new recruits. There were also fewer late entrants who held higher research degrees; thus one might con-

TABLE 5

Degree Level Attained

Year	B.D. %	M.A./B.D. %	M.A./B.D. & other %
1910	18·9	75·7	5·4
1920	6·8	84·1	9·1
1930	5·3	84·2	10·5
1940	3·6	75·9	20·5
1950	43·7	45·1	11·3
Total sample	16·8	70·3	12·8

TABLE 6

Degree Level of the Normal and Late Entrants in 1950

	B.D. %	M.A./B.D. %	M.A./B.D. & other %
Normal	11·1	55·6	33·3
Late	54·9	41·2	3·9
Total sample	43·9	44·9	11·6

clude that the slight increase of recruits who had taken further degrees have tended to be normal rather than late entrants.

Conclusions

What conclusions can be drawn as to the nature of the ministry and its implications for the church as a whole? Certainly the geographic origins of the minister have changed considerably over the last fifty years. The increasing proportion of ministers recruited from the Lowlands and urban areas may well go some of the way in explaining the difficulty now found in filling vacant Highland charges. In 1957 it was reported[27] that 80 out of 167 vacant charges were located in the Highlands. The Home Board[28] pointed out in 1965 that if there was any shortage of ministers it would be the rural areas that would most likely suffer. Fifty years ago, however, when the proportion of Highland ministers was still large, the church found it necessary to offer a £50 incentive to any minister willing to move south with the population into the cities and industrial areas. It is now suggested that the same incentive be transferred from these charges to the Highland charges.

The drop in the proportion of ministers whose fathers were themselves ministers raises serious problems for the church. Traditionally, self-recruitment was the means of maintaining a sufficient number of applicants for the ministry. It has now, however, become more and more necessary to institute recruitment campaigns to take over the role played by the ministers. No longer can the church be seen as self-perpetuating in its recruitment. The need now is to devise new techniques for drawing in applicants.

The educational patterns have perhaps the greatest implications for the church as a social institution. The trend towards increased selection from secondary schools is surely beneficial in that a wider section of society is being recruited than previously. Unlike the Church of England, in the Church of Scotland the tendency in recruitment is towards an open door policy rather than selection from a restricted educational sector of the population.

The drop in school leaving age, however, like the lowered educational qualifications, may well lead to other problems – mainly that of status maintenance. The ministry traditionally was respected as a high status profession – an assessment based far more upon educational qualifications than income (stipend). If the church cannot draw in well-educated applicants, educated not only at school but also at university level, can it hope to maintain its status as a profession?[29] The more important question remains, though, whether the status of the profession affects the status of the church as a whole. If it is the case that the ministry must maintain its status in order to earn respect for the church, the lowering of the educational requirements may have disastrous implications for the church. Certainly there has been an increase in the number of candidates who have taken only the modified course, a course that, as Whyte points out 'was never intended to produce a second class minister, inferior in any way. However it has been said and not without justification that the course is easy to enter and impossible to fail.'[30]

The implications of recruiting a larger proportion of late entrants may be seen in the increase in the age of entry. More candidates are recruited later in life, often already married with families. Not only is it likely that such ministers will be reluctant to remain mobile when in their career, but also will surely opt for charges with large manses and congenial surroundings for their families. Recruitment will become harder as the average age of the ministers is raised and the career lengths become shorter. More ministers will be needed to replace the late entrants sooner than would be necessary if younger ministers were recruited.

Many other problems may arise as a result of the changes in selection and recruitment of ministers, for only the most obvious are examined here. What is needed is more research, investigating the effects of particular changes in the type of minister, whether in terms of geographic origins or social and educational background, with respect to the particular problems the church faces as a social institution. It is important that the areas of decline, whether organizational or financial, are not explained away by the broad definition of secularization, for part of the cause and solution may well rest with the particular type of minister selected and the number of ministers recruited. The church, in its effort to adapt to a constantly shifting environment, must be aware not only of the choices open to it in terms of responses but also of the consequences of those responses. It would be futile if the church were to change its recruitment policy to alleviate the problems of reduced supply of ministers only to aggravate crises in other areas.

Appendix: The Survey

This study is part of an M.A.(Hons) thesis at the University of Edinburgh, 1972. The sample of 296 ministers was obtained by selecting one year in ten, i.e. 1910, 1920, 1930, 1940, 1950, and taking every minister ordained in that year. The names of these ministers were found in the ordination lists of the *Yearbook of the Church of Scotland* (1910-50), the rest of the data also having been collated from secondary sources.

(1) Curriculum vitae – the date and place of birth, father's title

(whether a reverend or not), name of school(s) attended and marital status were found in the individual autobiographies of the *Fasti Ecclesiae Scoticanae*.[31] The age of the minister at entry, ordination and marriage were calculated from the dates given.

(2) Education – information as to the type of school attended was found in the various official publications for the Scottish Education Department. The *Education Committee Yearbook* (1939-67), the *Education Authority Directory* (1903-70), *Schools* (1923-67) and the *Statistical Lists* of the S.E.D. (1923-67). The status of the last school attended was used, as indicated by the last year of attendance rather than its present rating.

(3) Geographic Origin – Scotland was divided into three sectors with the Highland-Lowland boundary joining Montrose to Helensburgh along the natural geographic fault, and the Lowland-Border boundary constituting a line drawn from Dunbar to Ayr. For the classification of those locations in counties neither inside nor outside an area but cut in half by one of the demarcation lines (such as Angus and Ayr), the co-ordinates of the site, as described in the National Ordnance Survey Map (1" to 1 mile, 7th series) 1961, were used to place it in the classification.

The categories within the continuum of rural to urban were classified according to the following criteria:

Rural areas	0– 1,000 population
Towns	1,000– 20,000
Large Boroughs	20,000–100,000
Cities	100,000 and over

The data was analysed using the techniques of statistical analysis on the computer package SPSS (Statistical Package for the Social Sciences). Percentage differences were used in comparisons involving variables rather than the actual incidence, owing to the sizeable difference between the different cohorts. In the 1910 cohort there were 36 ministers, in 1920, 44 ministers, in 1930, 45 ministers, and in 1940 to 1950 there were 90 and 79 ministers respectively. The data was statistically evaluated by means of the X^2 test.

NOTES

1. Membership figures consist of all those listed on the Rolls rather than the total attendance at services.

2. *The Yearbook of the Church of Scotland*, 1900-50.

3. Ibid., 1973, p.28.

4. *Life and Work*, May 1965, p.14.

5. D. Jenkins, *Gift of the Ministry*, Faber & Faber 1947, p.8.

6. G. D. Henderson, *Church and Ministry*, Hodder & Stoughton 1967. p.179.

7. Ibid., p.180.

8. Ibid., p.180.

9. J. Knox, 'The Ministry in the Primitive Church', *The Ministry in the Historical Perspectives*, ed. H. R. Niebuhr and D. D. Williams, Harper and Bros., NY 1956, pp.1-27.

10. Ibid., p.2.

11. Ibid., p.1.

12. J. Knox, *The Book of Discipline*, Leyden 1621. This is the official confession of faith of the Church of Scotland.

13. G. D. Henderson, op. cit., p.17.

14. J. Whyte, 'The Church of Scotland', *Preparing for the Ministry of the 1970s*, ed. H. G. G. Herklots, J. Whyte and R. Sharp, SCM Press 1964, p.89.

15. G. D. Henderson, op. cit., p.180.

16. D. O. Moberg, *The Church as a Social Institution*, Prentice-Hall, N.J. 1962, p.482.

17. The north region used in the census data is directly comparable to that of the Highland area used in the survey. The Lowland belt is almost identical to the aggregate of the east central and west central regions of the census data, the difference between the two not being significant.

18. In the census data, rural areas have a population of less than 1,000, exactly equal to that used in the survey. The urban area is therefore comparable to the aggregate of the categories of towns, large boroughs and cities.

19. D. O. Moberg, op. cit., p.483.

20. L. Paul, *The Deployment and Payment of the Clergy*, Church Information Office for the Control Advisory Council for the Ministry, 1964, p.275f., quotes the Fayers-Heawood Research (1954-62) which shows that 85% of public school candidates were selected in the Church of England, 80% from grammar school applicants and 68% from the secondary modern school candidates. A. Coxon, *A Sociological Study of the Recruitment, Selection, and Professional Socialization of Anglican Ordinands*, unpublished thesis, Leeds University, 1965, drew up the following statistics: 35% of his sample of ordinands came from public/independent schools, 43% from grammar, high and direct grant schools, and 22% from secondary modern schools. See also A. Coxon, 'An Elite in the Making', *New Society*, 26 November 1964, no. 113, pp.24-25.

21. Feepaying schools are distinct from public schools in that they are grant-aided by the government, while public schools are privately endowed. In terms of status ranking, feepaying schools in Scotland can be roughly equated with English grammar schools.

22. A Coxon, 1965, op. cit.

23. These late entrants were, however, exceptional in that they were forced into the army and could not, because of the War, qualify as normal entrants. How representative they are of the average late entrant really needs further testing.

24. Over the 50 years only 7 out of 273 cases, 2.6% of the total sample, married twice.

25. G. D. Henderson, op. cit., p.196.

26. The modified course was intended to serve for those who had missed the chance to get a degree but decided later to join. It was not intended as an easy way into the ministry for those who could have obtained a degree. However by 1959, the Education for the Ministry Committee reported to the General Assembly that it was beginning to be seen as an alternative to taking the arts degree.

27. Report of the Home Board, 1965, in Reports of the General Assembly.

28. Ibid.

29. For criticism of the degree of professionalism of the ministry see B. Wilson, 'The Paul Report Examined', *Theology*, vol. LXVIII, no. 536, 1965, pp.89-103, and A. Coxon, 1965, op. cit.

30. J. Whyte, op. cit., p.91.

31. *Fasti Ecclesiae Scoticanae*, ed. W. S. Crokett and F. Grant, Oliver & Boyd 1915-28.

7 Seventh-day Adventists and the Millennium

Robin Theobald

Millenarian movements have received a good deal of attention from specialists in various fields; as Wilson has pointed out, the study of such phenomena represents a convergence of interest by historians, ethnologists, anthropologists, theologians and sociologists.[1] Generally speaking, sociologists and social anthropologists have associated such movements with some form of deprivation, whether it be economic, political, cultural or some combination of these. Thus the peasants of mediaeval Europe; the new urban proletariat of industrial England; indigenous peoples under some form of colonial domination; these and other groups have looked for the fulfilment of otherwise inaccessible goals in millennial expectation.

But, as many writers have noted, intense millennial expectation is difficult to maintain over anything but a fairly short period of time. Such movements are thus particularly susceptible to change or disintegration. The massive disappointment at the failure of the messiah to arrive is often sufficient to ensure the movement's collapse. However, the non-materialization of the millennium does not necessarily threaten the very existence of a movement although in order to survive it may have to undergo something of a transformation.

This transformation may be far reaching in the sense that the movement ceases to be religious and becomes secular and, perhaps, political. Worsley, for example, tells us that in Melanesia 'a general trend' is for the cargo cults he analyses to move away from religiously inspired chiliasm towards secular political organization.[2] Indeed, Worsley and others have seen in millenarian expectation generally a force which can unify hitherto politically passive groups and pave the way for future political action.[3]

However, millennial movements which survive *qua* religious

movements tend, it is usually argued, to become more passive:

> The day of the millennium is pushed farther back into the remote
> future; the Kingdom of the Lord is to come, not on this earth, but in
> the next world; and the faithful are to gain entrance to it not by fighting
> for it in the here-and-now ... but by leading quiet virtuous lives.[4]

In fact Worsley seems to establish a connection between a movement's view of the millennium and its position on the passive-
active continuum. Those movements which view the millennium as
imminent tend to be much more activist than movements which
expect it to occur in the remote future.

However, such a generalization does not hold for all millenarian
movements particularly, it would seem, modern ones. Worsley
himself recognizes this with regard to Jehovah's Witnesses[5] and
Talmon[6] using Wilson's data on the Christadelphians[7] makes a
similar point. Although the Christadelphians live 'in tense expectation of an imminent and total redemption',[8] apart from defying the
authorities over the issue of conscription, as a sect they are essentially passive. Wilson himself suggests that this passivity may be
explained by the slender chances for staging a successful rebellion
in modern society.[9] Robertson, too, advances a similar hypothesis
for Seventh-day Adventists and Jehovah's Witnesses: these two
sects, he suggests, 'manifest somewhat less immediately-concrete
terrestial beliefs' largely as a matter of political prudence as they
wish to avoid a dramatic confrontation with the wider society.[10]

Such explanations may satisfactorily explain the passivity of the
Christadelphians and Jehovah's Witnesses but they do not, however, account for the passivity of the Seventh-day Adventists.
Indeed it would seem that the customary association of millenarism
with religiously inspired revolutionism[11] will, with regard to this
particular sect, serve only to obscure the real nature of its beliefs
and the consequent orientation of its adherents of the world. The
Seventh-day Adventists have a world-wide organization including
not only churches and schools but hospitals, sanitaria, publishing
houses, food factories and two universities. *The Seventh-day
Adventists Yearbook* carries advertisements for property and life
insurance.[12] Such extensive this-worldly activities are obviously
difficult to reconcile with what has been taken to be the characteristic orientation of adventist or millenarian movements, i.e.
hostility and withdrawal.

In order to clarify the present-day position of the Seventh-day

Adventists it is crucial to look at the development of the movement and the evolution of its beliefs from their origins in a wave
of religious revivalism which swept certain areas of early-nineteenth
century America.

The Development of the Seventh-day Adventist Movement

The roots of the Seventh-day Adventists movement lie in the intense
millennial expectation which was unleashed by the teachings of
William Miller, farmer and Baptist preacher of Low Hampton,
New York. In 1818, after two years' close study of the Bible,
Miller concluded that in about twenty-five years 'all the affairs of
our present state would be wound up'.[13] This prophecy was based
primarily upon the book of Daniel and particularly upon the verse
which states that after a period of 2,300 days the 'sanctuary' is
to be cleansed. According to Miller this referred to the cleansing
of the earth by fire at Christ's second coming. Arguing that the
2,300 days stood for years and that this period began with the
restoration of national government to the Jews in 457 BC, Miller
concluded that the second coming would occur around 1843.

By the early 1830s Miller was preaching full-time, lecturing,
and publishing newspaper articles all over small-town New England. From 1840 onwards Millerism ceased to rest upon the
activities of one man and became more of a movement. A significant development was an invitation for Miller to speak in Boston.
This led to the first 'General Conference of Christians Expecting
the Advent' held in Boston and the erection there of a tabernacle.
Initially preachers who had accepted Miller's teachings were per-
mitted to disseminate his prophecies from the pulpits of the established protestant churches, but as enthusiasm grew relations
between the Millerites and these churches were characterized by a
growing tension. By the beginning of 1843 many protestant ministers
were inveighing against Miller and denouncing his views as heretical. The movement also came under attack from sections of the
popular press who denounced Miller as a fanatic whose doctrines
drove people insane. Probably incited by such calumnies, mobs
tried to break up many of the Millerite camp meetings which were
held from the summer of 1842 onwards. But despite such attacks
the number who accepted Miller's eschatology continued to grow:
it has been estimated that at its height the Millerite movement

had a following of around 50,000 firm believers, with perhaps a further million who were interested though more sceptical.[14]

In his earlier sermons Miller had set the date for Christ's return at about 1843. In January of that year, however, he fixed the time between 21 March 1843 and 21 March 1844. After the passing of March 1844 there was deep disappointment among the Millerites, but this was overcome. Energy and enthusiasm were revived to such an extent that one of the movement's leaders was led to declare in July 1844: 'I have never witnessed a stronger or more active faith.' This phenomenon of the failure of prophecy leading to increased fervour and energy is not unusual. It is treated at length by Festinger and others, who cite the Millerite movement at this stage as a clear-cut example of disconfirmation of prophecy leading to even greater faith, in this case, in the imminence of the second coming.[15]

During the late summer of 1844 a new date for the second coming emerged from a camp meeting in Exeter, New Hampshire. Here S. S. Snow expounded his thesis that the cleansing of the sanctuary would take place on the Day of Atonement which he reckoned to be 22 October 1844. The adventists of New England seized upon this new date which transformed their indefinite though real belief into a belief so specific as to inspire them with a new zeal.

As 22 October approached enthusiasm reached fever pitch. Camp meetings became so crowded that they began to get disorderly. Extra issues of adventists newspapers were produced as well as pamphlets and adventist literature generally. The editor of the leading Millerite newspaper – the *Midnight Cry* – claimed that in order to provide the literature needed four steam presses had to be kept running day and night. By now the leaders of the movement were advocating the cessation of normal everyday activities in order that the faithful would have more time to spread the news. The closer the appointed day came the more the behaviour of Millerite devotees typified that of millenarian expectation generally. Work in the fields ceased, artisans closed their workshops and traders their stores. Possessions were sold and in some cases given away to the poor. Debts were settled and last goodbyes were said as the faithful retired to their homes to await the coming of the Lord.[16]

Belief in the second coming and the fixation on the date of 22

October was so intense that the distress following its non-materialization was too overwhelming for the movement to survive. Although it had survived previous disconfirmations of prophecy 'the Great Disappointment' of 22 October 1844 brought an end to the Millerite movement in its original form.[17]

An attempt was made to hold the movement together at a conference called in April 1845. But this conference became the scene of the internecine conflict and factionalism which, it has been noted, seem to afflict most millenarian movements facing a crisis of non-materialization.[18] Much of the dissension naturally centred upon the interpretation of the scriptures and particularly the time prophecies which had set the various dates.

Out of this controversy emerged three main factions, the first of which comprised the majority of the remnant Millerite movement including Miller himself. Their doctrinal position was that previous prophecy had been *invalid*; that the end of the 2,300 year/days was still in the future, albeit in the very near future. (Miller died in 1849 convinced that the second advent was imminent.) Accordingly, this group re-constituted itself as a movement in order that further evangelism could be undertaken. From it emerged the Evangelical Adventists, a body which survived until the 1920s. An offshoot, the Advent Christian movement, continues to exist in the US today.

A second faction, known as the spiritualizers or spiritualists, held that the Millerite prophecy had been entirely correct; that the second advent had actually occurred on 22 October but that it had been spiritual rather than literal. Many members of this group therefore believed that they had already entered the Kingdom spiritually. Consequently some of them refused to work, even to eat; some professed sinlessness, embraced celibacy or took spiritual wives; others went over to the Shakers. With such extremes of behaviour it is not surprising that this faction soon stumbled into fanaticism and disappeared.

From a third faction springs the present-day Seventh-day Adventists movement. What distinguishes this third group is that its members were able to re-interpret Millerite prophecy as being valid yet without putting themselves in the ultimately self-destructive positon of the second faction. A key figure in this re-interpretation was Hiram Edson, a Methodist steward who had accepted the message of the second advent in 1839. The day after the Great

Disappointment Edson was walking through a field with fellow-adventist, O. R. Crosier, when an overwhelming conviction came over him. It suddenly dawned upon him that 22 October 1844 marked the beginning of the cleansing of the sanctuary *in heaven* and not here on earth. Only when Christ had completed the cleansing of the heavenly sanctuary – what Seventh-day Adventists came to call the 'investigative judgment' – only then would he descend to earth.[19]

Edson's view of the cleansing of the sanctuary was published in surviving adventist newspapers and came to provide a rallying point for certain remnants of the Millerite movement who were attracted by this positive interpretation of prophecy. The result was a conference at Edson's home attended by, among others, Joseph Bates, an ex-sea captain turned preacher who had accepted Miller's teaching in 1839 and thereafter devoted all his time to the movement. Early in 1845 Bates had become convinced of the validity of arguments for observing the seventh day as the sabbath. During the conference at Edson's home Bates expounded these arguments with such lucidity that they were accepted by all present.

During the latter half of the 1840s this third remnant of the Millerite movement was able to consolidate its doctrinal position by means of a series of such conferences. A key figure at these conferences and in the Seventh-day Adventist movement as a whole was Ellen Gould White. Mrs White had accepted Miller's teaching when she had heard him preach in 1840 in her hometown of Portland, Maine. In the aftermath of the Great Disappointment she experienced the first of her visions in which she witnessed a representation of the travels of the adventist people to the city of God. Her experience was accepted by other Portland adventists as being of divine inspiration and she began travelling around New England relating her vision to scattered remnants of the Millerite movement.

There can be little doubt that Mrs White provided the nascent Seventh-day Adventist movement with the leadership needed to constitute it as an ongoing entity. During the all-important early conferences her charismatic personality was able to prevail over factional differences. When opinion divided over the interpretation of the scriptures Mrs White's visionary guidance indicated the true path. Under her inspired direction, what Froom refers to as the three basic strands of Seventh-day Adventist doctrine were drawn together: Edson's view of the sanctuary; Bate's seventh-day sabbath and what is referred to as 'the spirit of prophecy'.

The spirit of prophecy is seen to be the Holy Spirit working through a prophet of God's choosing. In Old Testament times and in the days of the apostles prophetical exegesis had been the accustomed procedure, but with the institutionalization of Christianity the practice had fallen into disuse. The Seventh-day Adventists came to believe that the spirit of prophecy would be revived during the the 'last days' – the unspecified period leading to the second advent. Mrs White was seen to be the prophet through whom the spirit was working.[20] Seventh-day Adventists hold that prophecy provides the key which unlocks the mysteries of time. The Bible is believed to provide the only satisfying philosophy of history; to indicate God's way out of the tragic morass of human suffering which the world has become. It is accepted as literally true being, in the words of James White, 'a perfect and complete revelation ... our only rule of faith and practice'.

Accordingly the Seventh-day Adventists believed that they had appeared at a time scheduled in the scriptures; that the drawing together of the three main strands of their faith at these early conferences represented 'a concurrence of fulfilments that could never have come about merely by human foresight and devising'.[21] Their historic role was thus consonant with the divine philosophy of history.

Having crystallized their doctrinal position towards the end of the 1840s, from the 1850s onwards the Seventh-day Adventists proceeded to consolidate themselves organizationally. In 1855 they moved their publishing house from Rochester, New York to Battle Creek, Michigan which became until 1903 the headquarters of the movement. At a general meeting at Battle Creek in 1860 it was decided to adopt the name by which they are known today. In 1891 the churches of Michigan formed themselves into a conference which led to other conferences and eventually to a general conference in 1863 at which the constitution was framed. The General Conference remains the basis of Seventh-day Adventist world organization today.

In 1874 the General Conference sent its first missionary to Europe, an event which marked the beginning of a world-wide expansion. In 1863 there were 125 Seventh-day Adventist churches with a membership of 3,500, mainly situated in New England. In 1971 the movement claimed 1,987,492 baptized adult members attached to 16,257 churches in 193 countries. The Seventh-day Adventists operate 46 publishing houses which produce journals, books and pamphlets in 273 languages. They are heavily involved in the fields of education, both religious and secular, and medicine, running schools, colleges, sanataria, dispensaries and clinics in most parts of the world.[22]

Seventh-day Adventist Eschatology

Seventh-day Adventists believe that on 22 October 1844 Christ began the cleansing of the sanctuary in heaven which involves an examination of the lives of all men through all past ages – the 'investigative judgment'. When the investigative judgment is completed Christ will leave the temple of God and will descend to earth to reward the righteous and punish the wicked. Christ's appearance on earth will be visible, audible and personal. His presence will lead to the resurrection of the righteous dead; a literal bodily resurrection which will mark the change from mortality to immortality. Seventh-day Adventists reject any notion of a spirit which survives death: death is an unconscious sleep from which the righteous will be wakened at the second advent. Immortality is, therefore, conditional upon righteousness.

After the resurrection of the righteous dead will come the cataclysmic destruction as foretold in the scriptures. Rebellious sinners will be destroyed by the fire and the sword of the heavenly host and all the work of men on earth will be annihilated.

Thus far the Seventh-day Adventist view of the millennium corresponds with the millenarian tradition generally, but from this point we encounter a significant departure. The righteous dead who will be raised at the second advent and the righteous living who will survive the cataclysm will then ascend with Christ to *heaven*. On this point Seventh-day Adventist doctrine is unequivocally clear: although a thousand year reign of Christ and his saints is foretold in the Revelation of St John the Divine there is no statement either there or elsewhere in the Bible that this reign will be on earth. Miller himself had rejected the idea of an earthly millennium with an elect ruling over the sinners. Seventh-day Adventists likewise quite explicitly deprecate chiliastic expectation which, they claim 'has been the root of doctrinal distortion, fanatical views, excess, totalitarian persecution and even political revolution'.[23]

The millennium is, therefore, the first part of the eternal state which is punctuated by the events surrounding the *second* resurrection at the end of the thousand years. This second resurrection will once more be bodily but this time will concern the sinners who had either not been raised at the second advent or who had been destroyed in the cataclysm. These sinners under the leadership of Satan, 'loosed for a little season', will attempt to take the city of God which has descended from heaven. However, the wicked will be extirpated as the very surface of the earth seems to melt and becomes a vast seething lake of fire. Then out of the ruins of the old earth will spring forth 'a new heaven and a new earth', a kind of pantheistic paradise graphically described by Mrs White as a state where

> The entire universe is clean. One pulse of harmony and gladness beats through vast creation. From Him who created all, flow life and light and gladness, throughout the realms of illimitable space. From the minutest atom to the greatest world, all things animate and inanimate, in their unshadowed beauty and perfect joy, declare that God is love.[24]

That the second coming is near the Seventh-day Adventists are in no doubt. An article in a recent issue of their major journal is entitled 'A Better World on its Way'.[25] This 'better world' is inconceivable, the article insists, without the return of Christ. It is important to note that since the time prophecies of the Book of Daniel are regarded as having been fulfilled on 22 October 1844, the Seventh-day Adventists no longer feel the need to engage in further date-setting exercises with all their attendant dangers: the second advent is simply imminent. To those who suggest that since they have preached Christ's return for more than a century the Seventh-day Adventists should give up and admit their mistake, the latter reply that the passage of time has only confirmed their beliefs. In support they adduce a number of world events which they claim to have predicted from a close study of the Bible. These predictions concern the increasing world turmoil – conflict, wars, labour unrest and the like – which is alleged to characterize the 'last days'.[26] As has been noted previously it seems to be a feature of adventist movements generally that they see in contemporary events a fulfilment of Biblical prophecy.[27]

The development of the Seventh-day Adventist movement and the evolution of its beliefs have been dwelt upon at some length in order that we may arrive at a proper understanding of the movement's position today. A key element in the preceding discussion is the rejection by Seventh-day Adventists of the notion of an earthly millennium where the unrighteous will be subjected to the rule of an elect. In this respect the Seventh-day Adventists deviate from the characteristic linking of millennialism with religious revolutionism. This deviation is all the more significant when we consider that the Millerite movement coincided with an international awakening of interest in the second advent, unleashed, it has been claimed, by the French Revolution in 1789.[28] Indeed, Desroche has argued that the Millerite movement was open to the influence of ideas whose origins lay in the events of 1789.[29] He is able to show that Miller himself was cognisant with the train of thought which saw the overthrow of the French monarchy as the prelude to the downfall of papal power (anti-Christ) which, as foretold in the scriptures, would herald in the millennium. Yet Miller emphatically rejected the revolutionary core of the political millennialism of 1789, while Mrs White saw its influence as being wholly pernicious, a subversion of God's will:

> When France rejected the gift of heaven, she sowed the seeds of anarchy and ruin; and the inevitable outworking of cause and effect resulted in the Revolution and the Reign of Terror.[30]

For Miller and other prominent figures in the Millerite movement the lawlessness and anarchy associated with the French Revolution were the direct result of the spiritual corruption which comes from disobeying the law of God. Consequently the notion of a revolutionary *bouleversement* was anathema to the Millerites with their emphasis on order, discipline and self-control: furthermore such a notion was not relevant to the socio-political conditions which inhered at the time.

Millennialism has previously been linked with the economic and/or political powerlessness (although some of the explanations in this vein have been criticized for their imprecision).[31] We do not know a great deal about the socio-economic circumstances of the adherents of the Millerite movement. Although there is evidence of disturbed economic conditions in at least one of the regions where the movement drew heavy support we cannot therefore assume that the bulk of its supporters were poor.[32] Although some were undoubtedly poor, others were moderately endowed traders, farmers and artisans while still others seem to have been fairly well-established members of the community. The movement was thus composed of diverse elements drawing support, as it did, from such varied areas as small-town New England, rural New York and such large cities as Boston, Philadelphia, Cincinnati and Montreal.

Just as there was no obvious all-pervading economic deprivation neither was there political deprivation: there was no oppressing class – no feudal landlords or colonial administration; in fact a salient feature of early-nineteenth century America was the absence of any stable class at all. In such circumstances the essentially political notion (i.e. concerned with the distribution of public power) of an earthly millennium was hardly relevant. What was relevant, however, was a system of ideas which provided stable values and a coherent philosophy of history in what was an extremely fluid frontier situation. Conditions in this part of America during 'the restless thirties and forties'[33] were those of rapid social change, of successive waves of immigration and large-scale movements of population to the frontier and to the expanding cities:[34] precisely those conditions which produce the anxiety and insecurity which in turn render individuals susceptible to emotional religious appeals. Given the inherent religious pluralism of the frontier situation – what Smelser has referred to as 'a free market in religion'[35] – such appeals were constantly made, Miller's being one of the more spectacular. It is generally recognized that in explaining the appeal of millenarian ideas cultural deprivation is often more important than economic or political frustration:

> Millenarism is often born out of a search for a tolerably coherent system of values, a new cultural identity and regained sense of dignity and self-respect.[36]

Just as an earthly millennium does not figure in Seventh-day Adventist eschatology neither do adherents of the movement see themselves as an elect. True the unrepentant will be extirpated at the second advent but they are only those people who have heard God's message but rejected it: 'No one will be arbitrarily excluded from salvation. The invitation is extended to all, but the decision rests with each individual.'[37] Thus the central goal of the Seventh-day Adventist world-wide organization is and always has been that as many people as possible, 'every nation, and kindred, and tongue, and people',[38] should be given the opportunity of hearing God's message before the second advent. Seventh-day Adventists state that they will never be satisfied until the gospel message has been preached to every person on earth; their target is, as the title of a recent article proclaims, the world![39]

Also relevant to their non-exclusiveness is the attitude of the Seventh-day Adventist movement towards other movements. Although deeply convinced of their unique role in the divine scheme of things, and to that extent distinctive as a group, the Seventh-day Adventists have for some time been firm advocates of religious toleration:

> We recognize every agency that lifts up Christ before man, as part of the divine plan for the evangelization of the world, and we hold in high esteem the Christian men and women in other communions who are engaged in winning souls to Christ.
> We recognize that the essence of true religion is that religion is based upon conscience and conviction. It is therefore to be constantly to our purpose that no selfish interest or temporal advantage shall draw any person to our communion, and that no tie shall hold any member save the belief and conviction that in this way he finds true connection with Christ.[40]

In effect, official Seventh-day Adventist policy on this issue extends beyond tolerance to active involvement in the struggle for freedom of religious belief:

> Church and state should operate in entirely separate spheres; we do not believe that in an attempt to control men's religion or religious activities the church should dominate the state, or that the state should govern the church.[41]

As part of its campaign for religious liberty the denomination publishes, in several languages, a journal devoted exclusively to this question.

Alongside its central organizational goal of proselytizing, the Seventh-day Adventist denomination has developed a deep involvement in a wide range of ancillary activities. Its educational activities, for example, are by no means restricted to the teaching of the scriptures but extend over the whole field of secular education. Its two universities in the US offer degrees in biology, business administration, English, history, music and mathematics.[42] Its home study institute provides courses in languages, science, history and business and secretarial education. The chief aim of these correspondence courses is to provide the student with 'credits'

– qualifications which may enable him to be occupationally mobile.[43]

The main impetus behind this involvement in the field of secular education is the belief that the individual has a firm duty to make the most of his abilities as exhorted by the scriptures:

> Each individual is first of all steward over his own being – his body and his mind ... A steward is responsible for the best possible use of what he has ... natural endowments and spiritual gifts or attainments are capital to be invested.[44]

Likewise it is the duty of the individual to keep himself healthy in body as well as mind, since 'God lays claim to our bodies. We are His by creation and redemption and He commands that we treat the body as His possession.'[45] Accordingly the Seventh-day Adventist movement has, from its early days, been preoccupied with the question of health and health education. As well as owning its own food factories the denomination publishes in several languages health journals which advise on dietary matters and warn against the dangers of tobacco, alcohol and narcotics. The Seventh-day Adventists also run anti-smoking campaigns.

Although the individual has a clear obligation to make the best possible use of his capabilities, this is in no way directed towards self-aggrandizement. Seventh-day Adventist writings are replete with warnings against self-indulgence, particularly against the self-indulgent use of one's possessions:

> As we view our possessions our question should be 'How can I best use all these things to serve my Saviour?' To disregard God's claim to our property and to use it simply as we please is robbery. We are accountable for all we possess, and we are to manage and administer it for the best interests of the One who has entrusted it to our care.[46]

> No man is valued for his possessions for all he has belongs to him only as lent by the Lord. A misuse of these gifts will place him below the poorest and most afflicted man who loves God and trusts in Him.[47]

The similarity between such exhortations and aspects of the system of beliefs alleged by Weber to constitute 'the protestant ethic' is quite striking as the following passage from the latter's essay demonstrates:

> Man is only a trustee of the goods which have come to him through God's grace. He must, like the servant in the parable, give an account of every penny entrusted to him, and it is at least hazardous to spend any of it for a purpose which does not serve the glory of God but only one's enjoyment ... The idea of a man's duty to his possessions, to which

he subordinates himself as an obedient steward, or even as an acquisitive machine, bears with chilling weight on his life.[48]

Such similarities are not so surprising when one considers that the Seventh-day Adventist movement is very much in the tradition of fundamentalist protestantism; in fact Schwarz has referred to Seventh-day Adventist beliefs as a 'modern-day version of the protestant ethic'.[49] He goes on to argue that a latent function of Seventh-day Adventist doctrine is to provide a framework of beliefs which is conducive to upward mobility:

> The dire Seventh-day Adventist predictions about the fate of those who fail to follow a rigid set of behavioural prescriptions are, in essence, an ideological support for persons who are trying to improve their socio-economic status against formidable odds.[50]

That Seventh-day Adventist beliefs may function in this way for certain adherents of the movement is perfectly feasible; but the size of Schwarz' sample does not allow us to elevate this connection to the status of a general explanation, relating these beliefs to certain positions in the socio-economic structure.[51] While agreeing with Schwarz that the tendency to include all millenarian movements under the revolutionary rubric may obscure more than it explains, the appeal of Seventh-day Adventist belief is undoubtedly much more diffuse than his analysis would imply. This is borne out by Borhek's observations based upon his own study of a Seventh-day Adventist congregation: his evidence suggests that the role-orientations of the members of this congregation fall into three basic types: doctrine-oriented, community-oriented and group-oriented.[52]

The doctrine-oriented role-orientation manifests a rejection of the larger community and hostility towards most other churches, especially middle-class churches. The basic function of the Seventh-day Adventist movement is believed to be that of saving souls and preparing for the second advent; evangelism and charity are emphasized. The doctrine-oriented tend to use the Seventh-day Adventist church as '*a vehicle of social protest*'.[53] The community-oriented exhibit acceptance of the world outside emphasizing education and social welfare. They are tolerant of other religious groups and see the Seventh-day Adventist movement as being most like the other liberal movements – i.e. Methodist, Congregational, Episcopal. As a group the community-oriented were distinctly better educated than either of the other two and their occupations were more prestigeous. The group-oriented are concerned with their own dignity and respectability as a group. They do not share in the egalitarian ideal of the movement and reject persons of low status. Members with this orientation, argues Borhek, tend to use the Seventh-day Adventist church as *'a vehicle of mobility'*.[54]

From my own observations of the Seventh-day Adventist move- ment – both at the level of local congregation and at the organiza- tional level – it would seem that Borhek's three basic role- orientations are useful in examining both the official stance of the movement and the appeal of its beliefs to various groups. Borhek suggests that about half the congregation he studied were doctrine- oriented, about one quarter group-oriented and the remainder community-oriented. It seems to me that the dominant orientation in any given congregation will depend largely upon the location of that congregation. Whereas the doctrine-oriented role-orienta- tion is clearly predominant in two almost completely black congregations in inner London, such examples represent one extreme of a continuum: to the extent that one moves away from such 'urban twilight zones' the pattern becomes less clear. It would therefore be foolhardy to attempt to formulate any general state- ment relating type or location of congregation to particular role- orientations.

However, it is suggested that the official position of the Seventh-day Adventist movement approximates closely to Borhek's community-oriented role-orientation. (It is significant that eight out of the nine respondents in his sample who exhibited this orientation were brought up as Seventh-day Adventists and attended Seventh-day Adventist schools, i.e. were not converted.[55]) Yet even within the official organization one is able to detect aspects of the other role orientations, particularly the doctrine-oriented role- orientation. This is evident, for example, in the different attitudes towards the anti-smoking campaigns which the movement is currently running in collaboration with Medical Officers of Health. Certain officials (the community-oriented) feel that it is the duty of Seventh-day Adventists to help people to try and stop smoking entirely irrespective of whether their campaigns yield returns in terms of converts. Others (doctrine-oriented) feel that this is all very well, but the movement's prime aim is to preach the advent message and win converts and that such campaigns should be judged in this light. That the former view has hitherto prevailed is indicative of the movement's overall 'reformist' orientation.[56]

And yet despite its emphatic disavowal of revolution, there is in Seventh-day Adventist doctrine a very basic appeal to precisely those individuals who are often seen to be the archetypal adherents of (revolutionary) millenarian movements – the dispossessed, the socially powerless, the rootless, the victims of rapid social change and so on.[57] This, I suggest, can be explained by the fact that Seventh-day Adventist beliefs combine a curious blend of intellectually disciplined ascetic protestantism on the one hand and a populist adventist fundamentalism on the other.

The Seventh-day Adventists have been described as 'the intellectuals of fundamentalism' whose beliefs are the result of 'alert, intelligent, inquisitive minds searching the Scriptures'.[58] Schwarz refers to the 'intellectual tone of their sermons'[59] and a recent exposition of their beliefs manifests a very capable level of biblical scholarship with references to such writers as C. Jung, Paul Tillich and C. E. M. Joad.[60] Yet this same volume carries a number of illustrations of truly infantile simplicity: Christ is shown, suspended by the gigantic hand of God, extending his hand to earthly beings: a smartly dressed individual is before the judgment seat accompanied by Christ who has his hand upon the former's shoulder; behind them an angel consults a weighty-looking tome and behind him, in serried ranks, a vast audience of angels.[61] Further examples of this very basic fundamentalism can be gleaned from the denomination's leading journal:

> When Jesus comes, grassy plots the world over will give up their dead ... Fathers and mothers with daughters and sons once more; lovers cruelly separated now united – what a day! Those arms will hug you again, those eyes will dance as before. So many of man's hopes and dreams are early dashed to the ground by circumstances or death. So many friendships are split by a funeral. But when heaven's paratroopers unlock the graves of earth, all things good and lovely are reunited – the future is open without end![62]

The presentation of doctrine in this form has an obvious attraction for the disinherited, the poorly educated, the deprived; those groups whose share of society's rewards is negligible and who are likely to use such a doctrine as 'a vehicle of protest'.[63] It is this aspect of Seventh-day Adventist teaching which accounts for the movement's extraordinary success, in certain urban areas, in attracting coloured immigrants. It seems that the Seventh-day

Adventist movement, although emphatically not pentecostal, fulfils similar functions for coloured immigrants as these latter movements have been observed to do.[64] As well as compensating for the various deprivations suffered by such marginal groups, e.g. conferring status which is denied in the world outside, such movements can also provide community-type involvement..[65]

We have seen that the origins of the Seventh-day Adventist movement lie in the adventist expectation of the Millerite movement. This movement, although millenarian, was also firmly in the tradition of fundamentalist protestantism placing great emphasis upon order, discipline and self-control. The idea, therefore, of the revolutionary overthrow of existing society was viewed by the movement's leaders, not only as anathema, but as wholly irrelevant to the world's problems.

The Seventh-day Adventist movement emerged from a faction of the above movement which was able to survive the crisis of non-materialization of the millennium by advances in scriptural exegesis. These advances not only were able to accommodate 'the Great Disappointment' but also, in avoiding further time-setting prophecies, successfully eliminated any danger of other such disappointments. The central goal of the nascent Seventh-day Adventist movement then became that of preaching the message of the second advent. Although this advent was and is viewed as imminent this has not led Seventh-day Adventists to adopt what has been seen as the characteristic response of adventist movements – withdrawal from the world.[66] This is to be explained firstly by the fact that the goal of proselytizing was supported by an educational programme beginning with the imparting of basic literacy but eventually extending far beyond this; and secondly by the doctrinal emphasis on discipline, self-control, bodily health and making the most of one's capabilities. These two factors combined have led the movement into involvement in a wide range of this-worldly activities. It is thus suggested that the official orientation of the Seventh-day Adventist movement approximates closely to that alleged by Wilson to typify reformist sects.[67] However, the central place of millenarian ideas in Seventh-day Adventist doctrine and especially their presentation is more in the 'orthodox' millenarian tradition.

The Seventh-day Adventist movement is therefore something of a hybrid, a factor that is almost certainly related to the somewhat exceptional socio-economic conditions which prevailed at its birth in this particular area of early-nineteenth century America. The uniqueness of these conditions is readily apparent from the high susceptibility of this region to numerous and often bizarre religious appeals: appeals as diverse as Miller's; the Fox sisters', whose adolescent pranks were responsible for the beginnings of the spiritualist movement; and that of Joseph Smith who in 1827 dug up the thin golden plates which, when translated, became the Book of Mormon.[68] However the fact that the Seventh-day Adventist movement departs from the ideal typical adventist movement does not in any way diminish its importance as an object of study. Indeed it is precisely such departures which enable us to elicit the essential features of such movements.

NOTES

I should like to express my gratitude to the staff of the St Alban's head-quarters of the Northern European Division of the General Conference of Seventh-day Adventists, and particularly to Dr B. B. Beach, for giving me much valuable information and allowing me access to their library. I should also like to thank Dr Bryan R. Wilson of All Souls College, Oxford, for reading an earlier draft of this paper and making several extremely useful comments. Naturally the responsibility for the views expressed here is my own.

1. Bryan R. Wilson, 'Millennialism in Comparative Perspective', *Comparative Studies in Society and History*, vol. 6 (1962-3), p.93.

2. Peter Worsley, *The Trumpet Shall Sound*, Paladin 1970, p.239.

3. Besides Worsley this approach is also very apparent in Georges Balandier, *Sociologie Actuelle de l'Afrique Noire*, Presses Universitaires, Paris 1963 and E. J. Hobsbawm, *Primitive Rebels*, Manchester University Press 1959. The following quotation crystallizes this line of argument: 'Millenarism, in fact, is not merely a touching survival from an archaic past, but an extremely useful phenomenon, which modern social and political movements can profitably utilize to spread their range of influence, and to imprint the groups of men and women affected by it with their teaching' (Hobsbawm, p.106).

4. Worsley, op. cit., p.239. See also Bryan R. Wilson, 'Typologie des Sectes dans une perspective dynamique et comparative', *Archives de Sociologie des Religions*, vol. 16 (1963), pp.56-7.

5. Worsley, op. cit., p.240.

6. Yonina Talmon, 'Pursuit of the Millennium: the relation between religious and social change', *European Journal of Sociology*, vol. 3 (1962), pp.125-48.

7. Bryan R. Wilson, *Sects and Society*, Heinemann 1961.

8. Talmon, op. cit., p.133.

9. Wilson, *Sects and Society*, pp.351-2.

10. Roland Robertson, *The Sociological Interpretation of Religion*, Blackwell 1970, p.166.

11. Wilson, 'Millennialism in Comparative Perspective', op. cit., p.93.

12. *Seventh-day Adventist Yearbook*, Review and Herald Publishing Association, Washington 1970.

13. LeRoy Edwin Froom, *The Prophetic Faith of Our Fathers*, vol. 4, Review and Herald Publishing Association 1961, p.463.

14. See Elmer T. Clark, *The Small Sects in America*, Cokesbury Press, Nashville 1937, p.45, and Whitney R. Cross, *The Burned-over District. The social and intellectual history of enthusiastic religion in western New York*, Cornell University Press 1950, p.14.

15. Leon Festinger, H. W. Rieckan and Stanley Schacter, *When Prophecy Fails*, University of Minnesota Press 1956, p.14.

16. See Froom, op. cit., p.882 and Cross, op. cit., p.307.

17. Froom, op. cit., p.827. See also Festinger et. al., op. cit., pp.22-3.

18. Talmon, op. cit., p.141.

19. Froom, op. cit., p.881.

20. Although Mrs White eschewed the title 'prophet', she nonetheless maintained that she was the messenger of the Lord and is recognized as such in official Seventh-day Adventist literature. See, for example, *Seventh-day Adventists Answer Questions on Doctrine*, Review and Herald Publishing Association 1957, pp.95-6.

21. Froom, op. cit., p.1048.

22. *Seventh-day Adventist Yearbook*, 1970.

23. *Questions on Doctrine*, p.446.

24. Ellen G. White, *The Great Controversy between Christ and Satan*, Review and Herald Publishing Association 1950, p.678.

25. *Advent Review and Sabbath Herald*, Review and Herald Publishing Association 1971, vol. 148, no. 17, p.6.

26. Ibid., pp.7-8. See also T. H. Jemison, *Christian Beliefs. Fundamental Biblical Teachings for Seventh-day Adventist College Classes*, Pacific Press Publishing Association, California 1959, p.332.

27. See, for example, Wilson, *Sects and Society*, p.231.

28. See, for example, J. L. Talmon, *Political Messianism. The Romantic Phase*, Secker & Warburg 1960, p.15 and E. P. Thompson, *The Making of the English Working-class*, Gollancz 1963, p.50.

29. Henri Desroche, 'Micromillenarisme et communautarisme en Amérique du Nord du XVIIe au XIXe siècles', *Archives de Sociologie des Religions*, vol. 4 (1957), pp.27-92.

30. White, op. cit., p.217.

31. Even terms like 'oppressed' and 'deprived' have been criticized as being too vague to avail of precise analysis. See, for example, Raymond Firth's contribution to a review article of V. Lantenari's *Religions of the Oppressed* in *Current Anthropology*, vol. 6, no. 4 (1965). See also I. C. Jarvie, *The Revolution in Anthropology*, Routledge & Kegan Paul 1964, especially pp.162-9.

32. Cross, op. cit., p.307, produces some evidence of an economic depression resulting in rural poverty in western New York at the height of the Millerite enthusiasm. W. W. Sweet, *The Story of Religion in America*, Harper and Bros. 1950, p.274, also talks, although in a somewhat vague fashion, about 'disturbed economic conditions' in this area during the same period.

33. Sweet, op. cit., ch. XVII.

34. Cross, op. cit., p.58, produces evidence of substantial population movement from New England to western New York between 1820 and 1835. See also S. M. Lipset, *The First New Nation*, Heinemann 1964, p.166.

35. N. J. Smelser, *Theory of Collective Behaviour*, Routledge & Kegan Paul 1962, p.188. Smelser suggests that such a 'free market' may be conducive to craze-like behaviour.

36. Yonina Talmon, op. cit., p.138.

37. Jemison, op. cit., p.225.

38. Revelation 14.6.

39. Article 'Target: the World' in *Advent Review and Sabbath Herald*, pp.20-2.

40. *Questions on Doctrine*, pp.625-6. See also Irmgard Simon *Die Gemeinschaft der Siebenten-Tags Adventisten in volkskundlicher Sicht*, Ascherdorf Münster 1965, p.211.

41. *Questions on Doctrine*, p.24.

42. *Seventh-day Adventist Yearbook*, 1970.

43. *Home Study Institute 1972* (A handbook of correspondence courses run by the Seventh-day Adventist organization), Review and Herald Publishing Association 1972.

44. Jemison, op. cit., pp.263-4.

45. Ibid., p.268.

46. Ibid., p.264. See also Simon, op. cit., pp.171-6.

47. *Questions on Doctrine*, p.564.

48. Max Weber, *The Protestant Ethic and the Spirit of Capitalism*, Allen & Unwin 1930, p.170.

49. Gary Schwarz, *Sect Ideologies and Social Status*, University of Chicago Press 1970.

50. Ibid., p.71.

51. This is admitted by Schwarz: 'Since my information is drawn from a small number of scheduled interviews which were definitely skewed towards the active, theologically articulate members of these groups, I cannot claim that my results are representative of these churches', ibid., p.183.

52. J. T. Borhek, 'Role-orientations and Organizational Stability', *Human Organisation*, vol. 24 (1965), pp.332-8.

53. Ibid., p.335.

54. Ibid., p.336.

55. Ibid., p.335.

56. See Bryan R. Wilson, *Sects and Society*, for a discussion of the main characteristics of sects of the reformist type.

57. See for example Clark, op. cit., p.255: 'Adventism is the typical cult of the disinherited and suffering poor.'

58. Introduction by a non-Seventh-day Adventist to a pamphlet published by the General Conference of Seventh-day Adventists, Northern European Division, St Alban's, Herts.

59. Schwarz, op. cit., p.138.

60. W. R. Beach, *Dimensions of Salvation*, Review and Herald Publishing Association 1963.

61. Ibid., pp.74, 234.

62. Article 'A Better World on its Way', *Advent Review and Sabbath Herald*, pp.6-8.

63. Borhek, op. cit., p.335.

64. See, for example, Clifford Hill, 'Some Aspects of Race and Religion in Britain', *A Sociological Yearbook of Religion in Britain 3*, ed. David Martin and Michael Hill, SCM Press 1970, and Robert Moore, 'In the Urban Twilight Zone', *The Listener*, vol. 75, pp.753-5.

65. See, for example, Gerhard Lenski: 'The successor to the ethnic subcommunity is the socio-religious community, a group united by ties of race and religion' (*The Religious Factor: a sociological enquiry*, Double-day 1963, pp. 319-66).

66. Clark argues that adventists sects are 'profoundly pessimistic ... The doctrine inevitably operates to prevent efforts for social betterment on the part of those whose dearest dreams are set on the second advent', op. cit., p.26. Froom discusses this assertion and concludes that far from being pessimists Seventh-day Adventists are 'true Bible optimists', op. cit., p.1005.

67. Wilson, *Sects and Society*.

68. Sweet, op. cit., ch. XVII.

8 The Swedenborgians:
An Interactionist Analysis

Robert Kenneth Jones

The most significant figure in the growth of the Society of the New Church, or the Swedenborgians[1] as they are sometimes called, was Emanuel Swedenborg who was born in 1688 in Sweden, the third of nine children in a pious Lutheran family.[2] 'From my fourth to my tenth year I was constantly engaged in thoughts about God, salvation, and the spiritual diseases of men, and several times I revealed things at which my father and mother wondered, saying that angels must be speaking through me.' He was a man of wide interest and imaginative insight, and at various times he sketched proposals for a submarine, aeroplane, machine-gun and steam engine.[3] He received his doctorate at the age of 21 and travelled abroad, spending a year in London and Oxford in order to improve his mathematics, physics and natural history.

His first appointment was as 'honorary Assessor' to the College of Mines which in 1724, when he was 36, became confirmed as that of ordinary Assessor, together with a salary. For the next few years he devoted himself to scientific writing producing *The Principia* (1734) and *The Animal Kingdom* (1743),[4] among others, all of which were sustained attempts to create a coherent philosophical basis for the natural sciences of the day.

However, this was the final period of his scientific writing. In 1743, when Swedenborg was 55, he claimed that he was subjected to a gradual revelation of spiritual insight.[5] The revelation came fully the following year: '(the) Lord Himself has appeared to me, and ... he has sent me to do what I am now doing.' He claimed contact with the Angel World, which was frequent and almost a daily occurrence. The spirits confirmed to him that drunkenness and homosexuality were 'enormous sins', and these same spirits are said to have constantly harassed him: 'Yea, also in the skin of my head, here and there with a slight hissing sound, like when some little distended visicle is perforated.'

This turning point, of 'amazing' gradual insights and spiritual conversion, made him withdraw from his work of Assessor in order to devote himself to the study of the Spirit World and the Old and New Testaments.[6] His programme of theological writing, which continued until his death, numbered 30 books, some, like his *Arcana Caelestia*, comprising several volumes.

Origins of the Sect and Schisms

In 1783, eleven years after Swedenborg's death in London, a certain Robert Hindmarsh gathered together a small group of five in his home in Clerkenwell in order to read the theological writings of Swedenborg. He had become aware of the work in 1778 when Swedenborg's *Heaven and Hell* was being printed by the firm for which he worked. Hindmarsh was the son of James, who later became the first of the new movement's ministers, relinquishing his post as writing master at the Methodist School, Kingswood School near Bristol, and ending his Wesleyan preaching. Robert was born in Alnwick, Northumberland, in 1759, and educated at his father's school. The small group which met in Robert's home developed into the first public meeting at the London Coffee House on Ludgate Hill. From there it adjourned to the Queen's Arms Tavern. It was but a short move to the establishment of a separate organization which called itself the New Church, the original name having been 'The Theosophical Society instituted for the purpose of promoting the Heavenly Doctrines of the New Jerusalem' (but in no way connected with Theosophy). The Great Eastgate Chapel was hired and opened for public worship on 27 January 1788, with James preaching the first sermon. Robert himself was later ordained and was a leading figure in the New Church movement until his death in 1835, being President five times.

At the time of the Clerkenwell meetings – and others held in rooms at the Inner Temple and New Court, Middle Temple – the group had not yet separated itself from the orthodox churches and denominations. But early differences in interpretation of the writings of Swedenborg, on which the new sect based its beliefs, soon emerged. This process can be illustrated by reference to John Clowes, who in 1769 became rector of St John's Church in Byrom

Street, Manchester. Clowes became influenced by Swedenborg's *Divine Humanity*, and translated it from the Latin in an effort to influence others. He used his Anglican pulpit as a platform for the new teachings, during the course of which he met opposition from members of his congregation. Hindmarsh wrote in the *New Jerusalem Journal*, 1792: 'Readers of the new doctrine are very numerous in and about Manchester, many of whom have lately come to the resolution of separating from the Old Church and forming themselves into a distinct body, openly avowing and propogating the doctrines of the New Jerusalem.' Clowes, however, was opposed to separation and believed that the new teachings would permeate eventually through the established churches. Although he made a special visit to London to plead his case to Hindmarsh and his friends the latter went ahead and formed a separate movement.

One of the earliest to come under the influence of Hindmarsh's public meetings was James Glen, a planter. Bound for New Guiana from England he broke his journey at Philadelphia, and in 1784 gave a lecture on Swedenborg's teachings. Swedenborg's works posted to Glen were later publicly auctioned and eventually led to the formation of a group of readers. The first American church was founded at Halifax, Nova Scotia, in 1791, and later groups were established at Boston and Harvard. This American development later became the General Convention of the New Church, a schism of the parent group in England.

The final schism occurred much later, in 1937, when there was controversy over the nature and interpretation of Swedenborg's theological writings. Over one hundred members resigned, chiefly in Holland, and formed themselves into a church body of their own which they now call 'The Lord's New Church which is Nova Hierosolyma'.

Order and Liturgy of Service

Molloy, writing in 1892, records that a service at Argyle Square, King's Cross, began with a voluntary on the organ 'during which the minister and his assistant, wearing white surplices extending to the feet and having voluminous sleeves, leave the vestry and take their places at the prie-dieus ... a hymn is then sung.' The service continues in an orthodox manner with the first and second lesson and doxology, prayers and further hymns, and ending with the sermon, hymns and prayers.

The origin of public worship in 1788 introduced numerous liturgical styles to accommodate the new movement.[7] Some attempts were made to form approaches to worship which were uninhibited by these liturgies but in a very short time, that is before 1800, several examples existed. The best known early liturgy is that of 1802 printed by J. Hudson and Co., but with an unknown authorship and possessing no Conference (the legislative body of the church) authority. The 1802 liturgy bears the influence of the Book of Common Prayer but nevertheless was primarily important in introducing the doxology into New Church worship. The 1820 Conference asked for 'a form of worship which would be less objectionable than any now in use in those Societies which at present prefer extemporaneous worship'. This led Hindmarsh and others to set up a committee in 1827 which in the following year produced a liturgy based on the draft of the form of worship used by Hindmarsh with the Salford Society. The 'old' liturgy made its appearance in 1875. One of the Committee members said that 'In three months the first edition of 3,000 was exhausted so I ordered 3,000 more, and then another 3,000.' This 1875 liturgy came under a certain amount of criticism. 'Conference, so often very wise, saw at once that any liturgy, because it will be used as a vehicle to take men and women near to the Lord in worship, must be treated with great care in criticism, and showed clearly that it did not desire to hear more of negative comment.'

The liturgy which is in present use made its first appearance in 1920, and is a revised version of the older one. Officially adopted by the Conference it is to all appearances a standard liturgical form containing the order of prayers before service, and the order of morning and evening services. The order of service for special days such as Ascension are set out, as well as the order of the sacraments for baptism, both child and adult, 'Holy Supper', marriage, burial, and specific prayers for the reception of junior and senior members, prayers for the sick, Te Deum, Psalms, and so on.

The Organization of the New Church

The first General Conference of the New Church (the legislative authority) met in 1789, although in 1821 it was reorganized as the General Conference of the Ministers and Other Members of the New Church signified by the New Jerusalem in the Apocalypse or Revelation of John.[8] The American Schism, after originally organizing in Baltimore in 1791-2, in 1817 adopted the name of General Convention of the New Jerusalem in the United States, although it was not until 59 years later that a form of worship was adopted in America.

Further internal controversy occurred in the American group in 1890 when the Pennsylvania Association, which consisted of 'fundamental Swedenborgians', insisted upon the virtual canonization of Swedenborg's works and withdrew when a motion to this effect was not passed by the Convention. In 1897 this Pennsylvania group broke away altogether and became known as the General Church of the New Jerusalem with a presiding bishop, a cathedral and college at Bryn Athyn. The College is called the Academy, and publishes the *Journal of Education*.

The Conference of the New Church, the parent British body, is the principal and original organization. The Convention of the New Church is the American group which is separately organized. The schism of the latter, which resulted in the Bryn Athyn community in Pennsylvania, has itself a smaller division on the outskirts of this community which is also separately organized. The Bryn Athyn group has its own schools and colleges and virtual monopoly over the commercial and social life of the area. There are societies connected with these sections in other areas of North America and in Africa, Australia and Europe. In Britain there is a small day school at Colchester. The Conference itself no longer organizes day schools. Affiliated to the General Conference of the New Church is the General Convention of the New Jerusalem in the United States of America and the Western Canadian Conference.

The Sections differ over the emphasis and interpretation given to the theological writings of Swedenborg, such differences resulting in the formation of slightly different organizations. However, these sections maintain friendly contact with one another, and in 1970 an Assembly was held in London to celebrate the 200th anniversary of the publishing of Swedenborg's *True Christian Religion*, which was attended by members of all sections from all over the world.

The *Swedenborg Society* was founded on 26 February 1810, chiefly by members of the Church of England who, having read Swedenborg's writings, formed themselves into a non-sectarian organization. It was incorporated in 1925, and is concerned with the promulgation, in definitive and scholarly form, of the works of Swedenborg, which have been published in English, European, Asiatic and African languages, as well as the original Latin. It also organizes lectures and meetings to promote interest in the work of Swedenborg. The International Congress of the Swedenborg Society met in London in 1910, and consisted of 400 representatives from 13 countries. Its counterpart in America is the *Swedenborg Foundation*. Both exist for the purpose of publishing Swedenborg's works which are the main-stay of the church, and both are staffed entirely by members of the New Church or its sections.

In Britain in 1965 there were 48 societies or worshipping congregations with a combined membership of 2,933,[9] and 15 study circles. In addition, there were some 400 isolated members who are catered for by a publication called *The Link*. Other publications which appear regularly include *The New Church Herald* and *The New Church Magazine*,[10] the latter being 'more scholarly'. The New Church also organizes an extensive missionary society, summer schools, correspondence courses, translating panels for the Old and New Testaments, and the New Church College, the last existing for the training of ministers.[11] There are 30 ordained ministers of whom 25 are in active service, 5 serving overseas. There are 6 'ordaining' ministers, 2 of whom are still active. The Overseas Mission Committee superintends the New Church proselytizing in Asia, South Africa (30,000 members), West Africa ('several thousands') and Europe, and the Continental Association of the New Church links organizations in Austria, Germany, Italy and Switzerland. There also exist other New Church organizations on the Continent as well as auxiliary bodies and societies.

General Conference (GB)			General Convention (America)			
1857	1900	1964	1850	1889	1899	1964
Members 3,000	7,333	3,772	1,450	7,025	10,000	4,831
Societies 48	76	56	54	—	—	65

The Nature of the Swedenborg Revelation

The Society of the New Church established itself as a new sect, breaking away from the existing orthodoxies, and in turn itself experiencing schisms because of the importance attached to the 'revelation' as manifested in the writings of Swedenborg as follows:

1. The Second Coming has arrived in the form of the new writings, and there is no other authority or law;

2. The former Christian Church is dead. 'Nor can there be a genuine Church except with those who separate themselves from it and come to the Lord in this New Church. The New Church is distinct from the Old, in faith and practice, in form and organization, in religion and social life.'

3. The Priesthood is the established means for the autonomous expression of the Church;

4. Baptism and Holy Supper and Conjugal Love are important components of the New Church.

The attitude to Swedenborg manifested by his followers is such as to suggest that he is regarded not simply as a man but as a divine manifestation comparable to that of Jesus as viewed in Christian orthodoxy. The 'Heavenly Doctrine' of the New Jerusalem as displayed by the writings of Swedenborg are 'Divine and therefore infallible authority ... (and one recognizes) ... these writings as being the Voice and Word of God Himself, and not of a mere man.'[12] In 1926 the General Church sustained this particular view by declaring 'This Second Coming was effected by means of a man, His Servant Emanuel Swedenborg, before whom He manifest Himself in person, and whom he filled with His Spirit, to teach the doctrines of the New Church, through the Word, from him.'[13]

The only serious contender to the paramount position of Swedenborg appeared in 1840, in a work entitled *Diary Spiritual and Earthly of James Johnston*, in New York. The original manuscript had been lost but a certain John Martin edited and subsequently published a diary version that he believed to be a valid facsimile of the original. Johnston records that 'Abraham met me according to promise, and amongst other things said he and St John would come on Wednesday and bring with me thirty-six kings'. Johnston's *Diary* is in accordance with the diary records of Swedenborg but, notwithstanding, this particular contender made little impact on the new movement.

The Doctrines of the New Church

The Word of God

The principle of Correspondence, a doctrinal interpretation of the Bible initiated by Swedenborg, states that the natural world corresponds exactly to the spiritual world. The Word has existed throughout time, and the Ancient Word was a source utilized by Moses to whom is ascribed the authorship of the Pentateuch. Before the Ancient Word there existed the Oral Tradition which accounts for the similarities in folk tradition drawn from many countries. The Mind of God corresponds to the universe which he has created '. . . the six days of creation corresponding to six stages in man's reformation and regeneration. The Levitical sacrifices, prescribed for ancient Israel in such careful detail, became, under the key of correspondence, a revelation of the spiritual offerings of the repentant life.'[14] The Letter of the Divine Word is limited to the books of Moses, Joshua, Judges, Samuel and Kings, Psalms and Prophets; four Gospels and Revelation.

The Second Coming

The Parousia is a spiritual event, as is also the Last Judgment. They are essentially past events which the New Church associates with the year 1757, when they believe the Last Judgment occurred at the 'end of the age' (Matt. 24.3), and that the Second Coming was effected through the instrumentality of Swedenborg. By this interpretation the Second Coming was into the world of Spirits because it was necessary that a human being from this physical world should observe and write about events in the Spirit world in order to convey his observations to mankind. The New Church believes that it was given to Swedenborg to be this observer and recorder, and that he wrote what he did without personal authority. 'The Lord has manifested Himself to me His servant and sent me on this duty.'

The rejection of Tripersonalism

The dissenting bodies of the eighteenth century, many of whom were influenced by the Age of Reason, often made a rationalistic restatement of doctrines and creeds. The various forms which the Protestant repudiation of Roman Catholicism took contained many elements in common but can basically be divided into two main streams. The first was that which adhered to the Nicene and Apostle's creeds, and the second was that which rejected these in an attempt to return to the primitive essence of Christianity. The rational climate set mankind firmly in a position to interpret the world around him. One of the dominant views of the eighteenth century was Deism which, proclaiming a natural religion, found no room for either the Incarnation or the Trinity. Many of the bishops and clergy in Britain were sympathetic to unitarianism and anti-Trinitarianism, and Freemasonry too had some inclination towards Deism. Reason became the paramount instrument of both the interpretation of the knowledge of God and of man's total cognizance of Christian revelation. It was in this context that the New Church rejected the view of the sophisticated doctrine of the Trinity established by the First Council of Nicaea in AD 325 in place of a theology of unipersonalism which members hold was precedented by Reason, the Old Testament and other great religions. It is in Jesus that the Divine Trinity of essentials, Father, Son and Holy Spirit, resides, and it is through Jesus's earthly life that the state and glorification is revealed to lead men to Redemption.

Heaven and hell

These are states or conditions. Death is a form of status passage from one form to another. It is a change of experience. 'Heaven is ... a real world, a beautiful realm full of men and women angels.' And those 'who are in heaven are continually advancing to the springtime of life; and the more thousands of years they live, the more delightful and happy is the spring to which they attain ... In a word, in heaven to grow old is to grow young.'[15] According to the New Church societies of angels vary, and some are concerned with the education of children while others are concerned with teaching those outside Christianity. Marriages are continued in heaven, if possible, and sexual intercourse is enjoyed not for the procreation of children but for goodness and truth.

The World of Spirits

The World of Spirits[16] is not the spiritual world, for the latter is the whole sphere of disembodied beings while the former is the area of those spirits who live neither in heaven nor hell but in between. In this respect it is similar to purgatory and the *kamaloka* of Annie Besant. It is a sort of antechamber that man enters into after death. Because it gives man the greatest possible freedom he is drawn to his 'real' abode as manifested in the fullest expression of his own inmost character. Female angels, characterized by their love of children, greet and prepare any of the latter who might enter.

The Nature of Swedenborg's Writings and the New Church Method of Biblical Interpretation

The New Church sees itself as the heralder of the new spiritual age of mankind, and it claims that its teachings have been revealed by God in the Writings of Swedenborg which contain a complete Christian theology. Considerable discussion has taken place by members of the New Church as to the exact nature of these writings,[17] and their interpretation is important because of the implication for the sect's teachings. Basically the position appears to be between regarding the writings as Divine Revelation (Swedenborg was God's human, expository instrument for interpreting the Word as contained in the Bible) or the Word itself ('dictated' by the Spirit of the Lord and exact to the very letter) which is limited to the portions of the Old and New Testaments mentioned above. Evidence from Swedenborg himself seems to suggest that the writings were from the 'Lord Himself' rather than from the angels;[18] that the complexity of the Apocalypse could only be revealed by 'the Lord'; that the nature of such revelation from 'the Lord'[19] has been granted only in this way to Swedenborg.[20] The implication from Swedenborg's own theological writings is that he nowhere claims that his writings *are* the Word – only the principles of the spiritual sense of the Word. The stress is on the newness of the manner of revelation.[21] Members differ on whether they believe the writings to be Divine Revelation or the Word itself. Swedenborgian fundamentalists claim that Swedenborg's writings are the Word because of two sections to be found in *New Jerusalem and Its Heavenly Doctrine* (section 251) and *Arcana Caelestia* (section 10320): 'What the Divine has revealed is the Word with us.' (Quod Divinum revelavit est apud nos Verbum.)

'The Word is Divine as a whole and in every part,[22] and the entire collections of sacred scripture were dictated by God.' As far as Swedenborg's own writings are concerned, a commonly held

view among members of the New Church is that the content of
the writings were given to Swedenborg by 'the Lord'; nevertheless
the choice of words was his own. 'His writings are truly the Divine
Revelation of the Spiritual Sense of the Word but they are not
the Word.'[23]

Swedenborg's approach to biblical interpretation was in keeping
with that of his age in regarding the testament as literal in the
historical sense. In this he differs from an approach which utilizes
merely allegorical parallels to the testament accounts. Members
of the New Church are not fundamentalist because they fully
realize the contradictory accounts which derive from a literal
interpretation. The Spiritual Sense of the Word was the result of
a non-literal interpretation contained *within* the natural world
and summarized in the principle of correspondences. Examples of
the Spiritual Senses exemplified in basic correspondence include
the following: 'When the head is mentioned in the Word, then
by the principle of correspondence, there is signified intelligence
and wisdom. By the eyes is signified understanding; by the nostril,
perception; by the breast, charity; by arms and hands, the power
of truth ... These correspondences of the body are built into the
language. We say that an intelligent man has a head on him, that
a perceptive man is quick-scented, that an intelligent man is sharp-
sighted ...'[24]

The nature of the visions

Swedenborg's conversations with the Spirits occurred not only
through the medium of dreams but also by 'changes in state when
(he) was writing. Afterwards there were many visions when my
eyes were shut; the light miraculously given; spirits influencing
me as sensibly as if they touched my bodily senses; temptations
also from the evil spirits, almost overwhelming me with horror;
fiery lights; words spoken in early morning; and many similar
events.' He was continually assailed by 'flames of various sizes
and different colours'. His initial interest in the natural sciences
was to enable him, so he subsequently claimed, to understand better
the later revelations. His writings after his dramatic conversion
were dictated to him by God. Some light might be thrown on his
experience and condition by his longstanding ability to retain his
breath for considerable periods without suffocating, an ability he
seems to have shared with several mystics and seers in history.

His initial vision and missionary institution were claimed by Swedenborg to have been given by God while he was living in London; and a person named Brockmer (living in Fetter Lane) recalls in William White's *Life of Swedenborg* the foaming at the mouth and stammering that accompanied Swedenborg's experiences. 'At last he said he had something to confide in me privately, namely that he was Messiah, that he was come to be crucified by the Jews.' The outcome of the behaviour was that Brockmer became frightened for his life and that of Swedenborg. 'While I was with Dr Smith (the physician) Mr Swedenborg went to the Swedish Envoy, but was not admitted, it being post-day. Departing thence he pulled off his clothes and rolled himself in very deep mud in a gutter. Then he distributed money from his pockets among the crowd which had gathered.' Although Brockmer met and talked to him on many occasions Swedenborg would never retract that he was Messiah.

An example of often bizarre visions included those of women, dogs and queens. 'I seemed to be with Christ with whom I conversed without ceremony. He borrowed a little money from another, about five pounds. I was sorry that he did not borrow it from me.' He appeared susceptible to visions even while eating his meals, and indeed his initial Commission was given in just these circumstances. He possessed a high sensitivity to bodily pains and discomfort which pursued him during and after visions, and also an apparent ability as a seer which is well authenticated. Many tales developed around his ability to predict events in the future and to 'see' events in the past.[25] Attempts were made to commit him to an asylum but to no avail. He died in London, where he spent his last days, in 1772, at the age of 84, having talked in his visions to Luther, Calvin, St Paul, St Augustine and Cicero.[26]

The background of the sect

The Society of the New Church bases the distinguishing characteristic of the movement on a rational approach to the 'Revelation of God'. One of the dominant theological ideas of the eighteenth century, Deism, was developed by such men as Edward Herbert and John Toland, who proclaimed a natural and universal religion, not mysterious but fully comprehensible by rational insight, and the Bible itself, formerly obscured in its meaning in many areas, was capable of clarification through this rational insight. The Swedenborgian movement emerged in an age in which the milieu was 'rationalistic', and in which mankind was believed to possess an inner 'faculty' of 'reason' or 'nature'. The seed had been sown in theological circles by the 'rational' theology of the Cambridge Platonists who emerged in opposition to the mechanistic materialism of Thomas Hobbes. The explanation of the hitherto mysterious resulted, according to the feeling of age, in a new knowledge of rational revelation, and those who adhered to this point of view were opposed to the emotional fanaticism and cant of many evangelical movements. Another source of influence, this time on Swedenborg himself, was most probably the Allegorists, and particularly the type of scriptural interpretation adopted by Sir Thomas Browne in the seventeenth century.

The Society of the New Church believes that the 'Spirit of the Lord' revealed itself to Swedenborg, who is regarded as the divine instrument through whom such revelation was given with the instruction to convey to the human race what was from that moment 'unveiled'. It believes that his experiences of the 'world beyond' were without parallel. By virtue of this special knowledge adherents, although maintaining that they are Christian, nevertheless place their emphasis on a *new* perspective of the *old* foundation, based on a rational and systematic interpretation of the scriptures by Swedenborg.

In a number of ways the teaching of the New Church differs from that of orthodox Christianity not only in its rejection of Tripersonalism for the belief that One God himself came to save mankind but also because it bases whatever doctrines it holds on the authority of the Word of God as defined by Swedenborg's explanatory doctrine on the grounds that the latter offers a model of rational faith. God's Will and Word is consequently believed to be revealed to men through the instrumental communication of Swedenborg's theological writings. The New Jerusalem and the life of angels has, for the sect's members, been graphically and immutably described by Swedenborg. Angels, for example, resemble humans in many ways except that their bodies are not material. However, they work, eat, copulate, and do all manner of things that humans on earth do. The central principle of New Church teaching is that of Divine Intervention by God himself.[27]

It is debatable whether Swedenborg envisaged the founding of a church after his death. 'Since the Lord cannot manifest himself in person to the world, which has just been shown to be impossible, and yet he has foretold that he would come and establish a new Church, which is the New Jerusalem, it follows that he will effect this by the instrumentality of a man who is able, not only to receive the doctrines of that Church in his understanding, but also to make them known by the press.' He claimed that true revelation had come from 'the Lord' and not from the angels, and he appears to have attested to knowledge by revealed religion sustained on rational grounds. The New Church, it is believed, was established to restore what Christendom had lost, and act as a carrier of new truths. The emergence of this New Church suggests no disparagement on the existence of any other Christian church '*so far as it is really the Lord's*'. It is therefore debatable whether Swedenborg wished himself to be seen as a founder of a new religious movement, and members emphatically deny that he *was* such a founder.

In most respects the Society of the New Church appears uninfluenced by other parareligious groups in the eighteenth century. However, some resemblances exist. For example, the early spiritualist T. E. Spencer's communication with angels is similar to that of Swedenborg, and Brook Farm, a socialist community connected with the spiritualist movement, was Swedenborgian. Various scattered interests in magnetism (animal magnetism or mesmerism), especially in Sweden, appeared to have been influenced by Swedenborg's writings.[28] Indeed, although the Society of the New Church condemns spiritualism, it has been argued that the sect helped spread the growth of interest in postmortem communication. Theosophy, with its roots in India, founded by Madame Blavatsky and Colonel Olcott, and whose leadership eventually passed to Annie Besant, has some resemblance in the *kamaloka*. The belief that humans have embodied the divine principle, for example Socrates and other sages, may have been influenced by the Swedenborgians. One of the first advocates of the New Thought movement, Warren Felt Evans, was a New Church minister. Christian Science also has some parallels, particularly in the prominence given to Mary Baker Eddy's *Science and Health With Key to the Scriptures*, and in the avoidance of words such as 'death' and 'to die'. In both groups members are referred to as having 'passed on', 'passed on to a higher life', 'passed into the spiritual world', and so on.

An Interactionist Analysis

The Society of the New Church is a formally organized religious movement which arose during the last two decades of the eighteenth century. Its origins bear out the conventional accounts of sect development, namely the presentation of a figure of some significance, in this instance *in absentio*, around whose new interpretation the first small group established a new pattern of worship and 'statements of belief'. The formal organization follows that of orthodox religious movements, with highly articulated decision-making processes available as part of the regulative machinery. The movement denies its sectarian character, maintaining rather that its role is somewhat akin to a new dispensation of the old Christian revelation. The fresh interpretation of Swedenborg's writings on the Bible is the basis of this new revelation. The Society of the New Church, as we have mentioned, was reluctant to disengage itself from the mainstream of orthodox Christianity in the early years of its development.[29] In its denial of its sectarian character and its reluctance to disengage it bears resemblance to another 'new dispensation' movement, the Catholic Apostolic Church or Irvingites. The Society of the New Church shares a variety of beliefs that mark it out as a transcendental value-oriented group, that is, as holding general, organized and existential value notions which influence behaviour by being concerned with substantive claims about the universe, society or the individual, such value notions referring to a super-empirical realm. Members share a variance of belief in a Second Coming, although in a retrospective and spiritual sense, and maintain their own peculiar interpretations of the Bible together with a concomitant regard for the writings of Swedenborg. An emphasis on the 'World of Spirits' further serves to donate the movement's sect-like nature. Its unique contribution, if we omit such groups as the Unitarians, is to offer a rational theology.

Movements as varied and dynamic as religious sects cannot be limited to a structuralistic-functionalist analysis.[30] They arise in, and are part of, a larger society. In the sense that the Society of the New Church differs from traditionally-sanctioned world views which are current in any given society it can be said to be *radical*, for a radical ideology *rejects* the taken-for-granted world view.[31] The adherent to a radical ideology adopts rigidly binding schema with which he interprets the world, and consequently the organizational task of the movement to which he belongs will consist of eliminating the possibility of derogatory significations of meaning being attached to believers' experiences. The three Parsonian variables involved here are: (*a*) gratification is commensurate with the movement's goals, i.e. members must receive a 'pay-off' in some form; (*b*) the internal structuring of roles must be so allocated as to minimize internal conflict and disharmony; (*c*) a relatively rigid boundary must exist between the movement and the outside environment, and this can be done by restricting interaction with the external environment and by monopolizing the interests of members.[32] Movements such as the New Church find an organizational solution by an emphasis on Swedenborg's significance and by the presentation of new information drawn from *outside* the realm of everyday life. They show an intense concern for the purity of the movement's beliefs (which becomes a means of control by the movement's leaders) and by a totality of concern in which the commitment becomes all-embracing, suffering becomes an integral part of the movement, and external affective attachments become minimized so that external sentiment becomes exploited for educational advantage. Radical ideologies will obviously not contain all these characteristics.

What has been said above must be taken in the light of the specific situational, interactive milieu in which such groups arise and are perpetuated. The New Church has a *meaning* which arises in the context of this interactive milieu as a function of three factors:[33] (1) the societal definition of the movement; (2) the adherent or potential joiner's own definition of the movement; (3) the movement's own or self-definition. In the first instance, any movement or group of the sort we are describing is regarded by society in a particular way. For example, it might be regarded as 'strange', 'freaky', 'hippy', 'weird' or 'occult', or it might be regarded as acceptable on a fringe level. The behaviour of the adherents may be such as to occasion no particular reaction in the external society because it falls within the bounds of normality or acceptability. Various combinations of factors enter into the total process. For example, the movement (and here we come to the self-definition) may not *care* what society thinks and may in fact thrive on its very rejection by that society. On the other hand, it might take great care to present an appropriately acceptable image. The movement's self-definition is the way that it perceives its role, which will in turn largely determine the formulation of the ideology, and vice versa. The adherent or potential adherent will, in turn, be a recipient of both the above definitions and his own definition of the movement will have to take account of these perspectives, together with the situational factors from which he originated.

To all intents and purposes the New Church *does* appear to have at least a part of its belief-system or ideology at variance with those in the 'mainstream' of society. The question remains as to how such an ideological variation can be sustained. Simmons' study of the Esper Community in Georgia[34] makes some important observations which could well be applied to any group entertaining an ideological variation. He lists five mechanisms which facilitate the maintenance of divergent ideologies: (1) selective attention is paid to those perceptions which are congruent with one's own beliefs; (2) social situations are actively structured so that their outcomes support one's own beliefs; (3) ambiguous evidence is *interpreted* as confirming one's beliefs; (4) social insulation of members and a rejection of non-members with different beliefs; (5) there is a marked ambivalence of the divergent larger culture towards one's beliefs.[35] By such mechanisms the esoteric elements in the doctrines of the New Church are sustained, and also those of such groups as the Christian Scientists, Jehovah's Witnesses and Mormons. Unless, as in the embryonic stages of these groups, the ideological divergence threatens the larger society, an ambivalent attitude will be entertained by the latter.

Salient Aspects of Social Interaction in an Analysis of the New Church

A group such as the New Church requires a sociological analysis which utilizes perspectives such as fluidity, dynamism and variance, and cannot be limited to a structuralist-functionalist perspective. Because 'reality is socially defined' such definitions are embodied in concrete and observable instances such as groups and movements in some form of social interaction. Furthermore, in order to understand how it is that a group or movement socially constructs its universe 'at any given time, or its change over time, one must understand the social organization that permits the definers to do their defining'.[36]

The movement under discussion, inasmuch as it adopts as 'morally' binding an internally consistent schema of interpretation, is in consequence 'marked-off' from the taken for granted world view. The Society of the New Church lends itself to an inter-actionist analysis which demonstrates a common ground for the organization of experience arising from an interpretation of the everyday world. The movement has an attitude of deep reverence underlying both itself and its creed, although such reverence is attached to a dead person and transferred to his writings. Such writings are a clear example of a 'new' knowledge received from outside the realm of everyday life. The movement has traditionally exhibited a deep concern for the purity of its beliefs, and it exerts a form of control by reference to the interpretation of Sweden-borg's writings. When we realize that these writings have been translated from eighteenth-century Latin the problem of inter-pretation becomes crucial. The Swedenborg Society, too, controls the ideology of the movement to some extent by having a monopoly of the publishing of Swedenborg's works. The American and Dutch schisms became simultaneously examples of this purity and aids to a crystallization of orthodoxy. In common with other sectarian groups the New Church's members exhibit a *totality of concern*, and suffering for the 'cause' becomes possible by the surrender of particular behaviour associated with the 'pursuits of the flesh of the world'. The movement implicitly legislates the number of external effective attachments which are allowed by organizing a full programme of social functions and activities, including an intellectual stimulus provided by the Swedenborg Society. The New Church possesses a number of well-defined objectives or goals, with a clearly recognizable organization, structure and leadership of priests.

The aetiology of the sect arose from interaction between an interest group and its social milieu. The writings of Swedenborg, recognized by Hindmarsh and his friends as possessing some special merit, became the basis of the new faith. In consequence, the movement sees itself as the inheritor of the visions of a man of great scientific genius, and this perspective conditions not only how society views the movement (some of the academic respect-ability of Swedenborg 'rubs off' on the members) but also how members see the movement. The ideology of the sect in time becomes an index of social perception that offers a map of social reality for the movement's members.[37] The present state of the movement suggests that the majority of its members are born into it rather than becoming voluntary members and the total missionary activity, or 'canvassing', for 1971 produced only 38 members, compared with 92 deceased and 73 'removed'. Membership is predominantly lower middle to middle class, with quite a number of nobility, medical men and graduates interspersed. There is no doubt that the movement is declining, but this is not seen as a cause for despair. Because it offers no cogent threat the movement is treated with a marked tolerance and ambivalence by society. The ideology of the New Church contains the same presuppositions[38] which underlie all ideological assertions, that is, these assertions are statements about the world which are answers to questions stated or unstated, tacit or assumed.

We have argued that the rise of the Swedenborgians was set firmly in the social and intellectual milieu of the time. Reluctant at first, and uncertain of its real mission, it resisted pressure to remain within orthodox Christendom. However, its form of liturgy and worship owe a heavy debt to the mainstream tradition. The emphasis placed on the revelation of 'the Lord' to Swedenborg and the credence given to the latter's heavenly doctrines produced a distinctive set of beliefs which mark the movement off. The intellectual and theological climate of the eighteenth century, with the influence of Deism, rational faith and theology, influenced the perspectives adopted by the sect to no small degree. Swedenborg was consequently credited with a charismatic revelation, and his writings regarded as containing a form of extra-terrestial knowledge. The nuances of Latin translation and subsequent interpretation have been a means of maintaining a purity of belief, and the American and Dutch schisms have merely served to crystallize the distinctive beliefs of the 'main' body. The use of an interaction analysis suggests that a group such as this can be regarded as having quite separate meanings for its members than it apparently does for the rest of society. Small and distinctive, its ideology nevertheless contains a clear statement of how the members 'map' the everyday world.

In some senses the movement we have looked at is at variance with the prevailing culture. Nonetheless, it is accommodated by, and in turn accommodates itself to, the prevailing culture because in the last analysis it offers, essentially, no real threat. To its adherents the ideology is a way of living, of carving out a distinctive course through the world. Such groups also possess ideologies which have arisen from a certain social milieu. Adherents may rarely recognize that they are engaged in acting out an ideology, for this is left to the observer who is himself uninvolved in such a task.

NOTES

1. As far as I am aware no sociological work has appeared on the New Church. I have drawn on accounts of the movement from the following mainly historical reference. L. B. De Beaumont, *Spiritual Reconstruction and the Religious Unrest of the Age*, 1918; J. S. Bogg, *A Glossary: or, a Meaning of Scientific Terms and Phrases used by Swedenborg in his Theological Writings, Given in his Own Words*, Swedenborg Society 1915; *Life of Swedenborg* (revised by H. G. Drummond), New Church Press Ltd 1956; H. G. Drummond, *Degrees*, 1908; Charles W. Ferguson, *The Confusion of Tongues*, Heinemann 1929, pp.240-364; *The General Conference of the New Church Year Book*, General Conference of the New Church, London 1971-2; John Goddard, *Wright and Wrong Unveilings of the Spiritual World*, NY 1912; *Encyclopedia of Religion and Ethics*, ed. James Hastings, New York 1922 (article on 'Swedenborgians'); Alan Grange, *The Structure of New Church Teaching*, Missionary Society of the New Church, London 1963; Helen Keller, *My Religion*, New York 1927; J. F. Molloy, *The Faiths of the People*, vol. 2, London 1892; Dradoba Pandurung, *Reflections Respecting the Doctrines of the New Jerusalem Church*, 1879; T. Parson, *Outlines of the New Religion and Philosophy of Swedenborg*, 1876; Cyriel O. Sigstedt, *The Swedenborg Epic: the Life and Works of Emanuel Swedenborg*, Twayne, NY 1952; Julian K. Smith and William Winsch, *The Gist of Swedenborg*, J. B. Lippincott, Philadelphia 1920.

2. The family circle included the outstanding theologians of the day such as Bebel, professor of theology and church history at Strasburg, Sebastian Schmidius, translator of the Bible published at Strasburg in 1696, and Clodius, Hannekenius and Arcularius.

3. His list of fourteen inventions included also a syphon, a sluice plan, a water-clock, a universal musical instrument and an air gun.

4. His publications were many, and included *The First Principles of Natural Things* (1734), *The Brain* (1742), and *Rational Psychology* (1742). From time to time he also read 'Memorials' to the Swedish Diet concerned with the finances of Sweden, a plea for establishing rolling mills, and so on.

5. This is a gradual conversion, or what Berger calls *alternation*, by no means an unusual occurrence but one which exhibits much less drama than conversion of a sudden variety.

6. Swedenborg also occasionally returned to secular activities, when for example in 1759 he read a Memorial for a return to a pure metallic currency. It was not long before the 'Servant of the Lord Jesus Christ' had two attempts made on his life.

7. I am indebted to the Rev. C. H. Presland, Secretary to the New Church Conference, for supplying me with information relevant to this section. The source of this paragraph is a mimeographed sheet written by him. I alone am responsible for the interpretation.

8. 'And I, John, saw the Holy City, New Jerusalem, coming down from heaven' (Rev. 21.2). The prerequisite for membership of the organization of the New Church is public profession 'of the Lord Jesus Christ as the only God of heaven and earth ... [and the members'] intention with His help to live a life according to the Ten Commandments as His Laws.' Swedenborg states that the quotation from Revelation 'signifies the New Church to be established by the Lord at the end of the former church, which will be consociated with the New Heaven in Divine truths as to doctrine and as to life' (*Apocalypse Revealed*, no. 871).

9. Mrs M. L. Friend, manager of the New Church Press, has assisted me in piecing together these facts, although naturally the final form is my own.

10. The New Church, operating from the same address as the former, in addition to the church's advertising, publishes a certain amount of material. This bears out the pattern suggested by other sects, for example the Catholic Apostolic Church, the Exclusive Brethren, and the Witnesses. *The Link*, servicing 'isolated numbers' and 'associates' of which there were 470 addresses in the Register in 1971, is also published by the New Church Press.

11. Apart from the programme of conventional missionary activity, the New Church has recently embarked upon a publicity campaign which consisted of five advertisements in *The Sunday Times*. For an outlay of £52, eight replies were received from Great Britain and one from Rome. Attempts have been made to sell copies of Swedenborg's writings at 'Pop' Festivals and an approach was made to the 'Free Communications Group', a commercial radio venture, which was discontinued when it was discovered that the aims of the radio group were not in sympathy with those of the New Church. The New Church is also engaged upon a complete translation of the Old Testament (now finished) and the New Testament. It also numbers among its organization the New Church Sunday School Union (1,099 children), the New Church Federation which is a youth movement with its own publication (*The Plough*), an orphanage, and the Women's League.

12. *Bryn Athyn and the Academy of the New Church*, Bryn Athyn, Pa. 1903, p.27.

13. *A Brief Handbook of Information Concerning the Bryn Athyn Cathedral*, Bryn Athyn, Pa. 1926, p.37.

14. Alan Grange, *Why the New Church is New*, Scottish Association of the New Church (pamphlet).

15. Swedenborg, *Heaven and Hell*, no. 414.

16. In many ways New Church doctrines, especially in an area such as this, laid the foundations for New Thought and Spiritualism (see below). Warren Felt Evans, one of the first advocates of the New Thought, was a New Church minister, and Thomas Lake Harris, the founder of the Brotherhood of the New Life, was a former Swedenborgian minister.

17. I am relying heavily on Alan Grange, *The Structure of New Church Teaching*, pp.123-39, for what follows.

18. Swedenborg, *True Christian Religion*, nos. 779-80.

19. Swedenborg, Preface to *Apocalpse Revealed*.

20. Swedenborg, *Invitation to the New Church*, posthumous publication, sections 43 and 52.

21. Alan Grange, op. cit., *passim*.

22. Swedenborg, *The New Jerusalem and its Heavenly Doctrines*, section 252.

23. Alan Grange, op. cit., p.131.

24. Ibid., p.71.

25. Swedenborg's 'Intercourse with the Spiritual World' are alleged to be attested many times, and the best known are The Case of the Stockholm Fire (which Swedenborg 'saw' with remarkable accuracy); The Receipt in the Bureau (when Swedenborg directed the searchers, again with remarkable accuracy, to a lost receipt belonging to the late M. de Marteville); The Dowager Queen of Sweden (when Swedenborg related a conversation which was known only to the Dowager and the dead Prince Royal of Prussia). New Church members are careful to point out that the truth of Swedenborg's writings is not dependent on these 'miracles'. The artist William Blake was a Swedenborgian for a time, and his work displays a visionary insight akin to Swedenborg's own.

26. As late as 1909 Swedenborg's remains were transported by train to Dartmouth and then on the *Fylgia* to Carlscrona. His remains now reside in Uppsala Cathedral.

27. Servetus, burned by Protestants in 1553, pre-empted many of Swedenborg's ideas.

28. Geoffrey K. Nelson, *Spiritualism and Society*, Routledge & Kegan Paul 1969, pp.20, 50-4.

29. J. F. Molloy, op. cit., p.32.

30. See a similar argument in Robert H. Lauer, 'Social Movements: an Interactionist Analysis', *The Sociological Quarterly*, 1972, pp.315-28, especially p.315.

31. Egon Bittner, 'Radicalism and the Organisation of Radical Movements', *American Sociological Review*, vol. 28, no. 6, December 1963, pp.928-40.

32. Ibid.

33. Lauer, op. cit.

34. J. L. Simmonds, 'On Maintaining Deviant Belief Systems: a Case Study', *Social Problems*, vol. 2, no. 3, 1964, pp.250-6.

35. Ibid., p.256.

36. Peter Berger and Thomas Luckman, *The Social Construction of Reality*, NY, Doubleday 1966, p.107.

37. Bernard O. Brown, 'An Empirical Study of Ideology in Formation', *Review of Religious Work*, 1968, vol. 9, part 2, pp.79-87.

38. R. G. Collingwood, *Metaphysics*, Clarendon Press 1940, pp.21ff. Collingwood held that presuppositions underlie the external world. All statements, whether everyday or contained within an elaborate ideological structure, answer questions which themselves arise out of these presuppositions. Such presuppositions are relative, and historically influenced, and at times they are 'consupponible', that is, because they sometimes conflict it is also possible to hold them simultaneously. In this sense deviant or minority beliefs can be adhered to which appear at variance with beliefs and knowledge about the 'real world' because each condition which gives rise to a different presupposition has its own distinction.

9 Bibliography of Work in the Sociology of British Religion, 1973 Supplement

Ronald Iphofen and James Edmiston

This is the fifth supplement to a bibliography initially produced by David Martin in *A Sociology of English Religion*, SCM Press 1967. Again the bibliography relies on empirical work which reflects the contemporary religious situation in Great Britain, with historical information added selectively. The co-operation of those who send us details of their research and publication is appreciated, and greatly facilitates the task of compilation. Correspondence should be addressed to Robert W. Coles, Sociology Department, University of York.

1. GENERAL SURVEYS AND COMMENTS ON RELIGION AND SOCIETY

Austin, W. H., 'Religious Commitment and the Logical Status of Doctrines', *Religious Studies*, 9, pp.39-48, March 1973.

Brown, J. P., 'Disestablishment: Christianity in Wales', *New Blackfriars*, 54, pp.19-29, January 1973.

Campbell, Colin, and Coles, Robert W., 'Religiosity, Religious Affiliation and Religious Belief: The Exploration of a Typology', *Review of Religious Research*, vol. 14, no. 3, pp.151-7, Spring 1973.

Currie, R., 'A statistical survey of religion in Britain and Ireland', Wadham College, Oxford University.

Dally, Ann, 'Backlash to established views', *New Humanist*, 88, pp.331-2, December 1972.

Duffy, Paul, 'How Institutions Change', *Month*, 5, pp.112-15, April 1972.

Figes, Eva, 'Doomsday doublethink', *New Humanist*, 88, p.22, May 1972.

Forster, P. G., 'Secularization in the English Context: some conceptual and empirical problems', *Sociological Review*, 20, pp.153-68, May 1972.

Goodridge, R. M., 'The Secular Practice and the Spirit of Religion', *Social Compass*, XX, 1, pp.19-30, 1973.

Harris, E. E., 'Reasonable Belief', *Religious Studies*, 8, pp.257-67, September 1972.

Hebblethwaite, P., 'What comes after secularisation?', *Month*, 6, pp.207-11, June 1973.

Hill, M., *The Religious Order*, Heinemann 1973.

Jerman, B., 'Diary dates in church', *Daily Telegraph Magazine*, p.7, 18 April 1973.

Ling, T., 'Religion in England: majorities and minorities', *New Community*, 2, pp.117-24, Spring 1973.

Martin, D., 'The secularisation question', *Theology*, 76, pp.81-7, February 1973.

Morris, J., 'Sex discrimination in the Church', *Month*, 6, pp.181-2, May 1973.

Nash, Daphne, 'Women's Liberation and Christian Marriage', *New Blackfriars*, 53, pp.196-205, May 1972.

Nelson, G. K., and Clews, R. A., 'Geographical mobility and religious behaviour', *Sociological Review*, 21, pp.127-35, February 1973.

Norman, E., 'Middle-class Christianity', *Spectator*, pp.665-6, 28 October 1972.

Orr, J. M., 'A difficult world to understand: a dialogue sermon', *Expository Times*, 83, pp.275-7, June 1972.

Peabody, S. B., 'Church's tremendous influence on life of the nation', *The Times*, 17 April 1973.

Schaeffer, F. A., *The Church at the End of the Twentieth Century*, Norfolk Press 1970.

Streib, G. F., 'Attitudes of the Irish toward Changes in the Catholic Church', *Social Compass*, XX, 1, pp.49-71, 1973.

Sturch, R. L., 'God and Probability', *Religious Studies*, 8, pp.351-4, December 1972.

Torrance, T. F., 'The Church in an era of scientific change', *Month*, 6, pp.136-42, April 1973.

'The Church in an era of scientific change', *Month*, 6, pp.176-80, May 1973.

Wilson, G., 'Why are Christians prejudiced?', *New Society*, pp.617-19, 14 June 1973.

2. HISTORICAL BACKGROUND (a selection)

Bocock, R. J., 'Anglo-Catholic Socialism: A Study of a Protest Movement within a Church', *Social Compass*, XX, pp.31-48, 1973.

Chadwick, O., *The Victorian Church, Part II: 1860-1901*, Oxford University Press 1970.

Fairfield, L. P., 'John Bale and the development of Protestant hagiography in England', *Journal of Ecclesiastical History*, 24, pp.145-60, April 1973.

Hunt, A., 'Hie thee hence', *New Society*, p.92, 12 July 1973.

Knox, R. B., 'Church history and the Church', *United Reformed Church Historical Society Journal*, 1, pp.4-9, May 1973.

Pickering, W. S. F., 'Abraham Hume (1814-1884), A Forgotten Pioneer in Religious Sociology', *Archives de Sociologie des Religions*, no. 33, pp.33-48, January-June 1972.

Prais, S. J., 'Synagogue Statistics and the Jewish Population of Great Britain, 1900-70', *The Jewish Journal of Sociology*, vol. XIV, 2, pp.215-28, December 1972.

Sharot, S., 'Religious Change in Native Orthodoxy in London, 1870-1914: The Synagogue Service', *The Jewish Journal of Sociology*, vol. XV, 1, pp.57-78, June 1973.

3. COMMUNITY AND PARISH STUDIES

Harrison, P., 'The Church and the city', *New Society*, pp.201-3, 26 July 1973.

Kerr, F., 'Communes and Communities', *New Blackfriars*, vol. 53, no. 628, pp.388-98, September 1972.

Spencer, A. E. C. W., 'The Catholic community as a British melting pot', *New Community*, 2, pp.125-31, Spring 1973.

Waterman, P., 'Milton Keynes and the Churches' Role in the Community', *Crucible*, pp.206-11, January-February 1973.

4. RELIGION AND EDUCATION

Hornsby-Smith, M. P., 'A sociological case for Catholic schools', *Month*, 5, pp.298-304, October 1972.

Jones, C., 'Religious Education in state schools', *New Humanist*, 88, pp.327-8, December 1972.

Kerr, J., 'Catholic Schools in Scotland', *New Humanist*, 88, pp.240-1, October 1972.

Knight, P., 'The case against Church schools', *New Humanist*, 88, pp.484-6, April 1973.

Norman, E., 'Christianity in the Schools', *Spectator*, p.1006, 23 December 1972.

Shackle, E., 'On teaching religion in school', *New Blackfriars*, 54, pp.81-6, February 1973.

Whitfield, G., 'Parliament, the Church and Education', *Crucible*, pp.172-5, November-December 1971.

5. RELIGION AND POLITICS

Doyle, P. J., 'Religion, politics and the Catholic working class', *New Blackfriars*, 54, pp.218-25, May 1973.

Howard, F., and Fuchs, F., 'Northern Ireland: What the clerics say', *Spectator*, pp.111-12, 22 January 1972.

Morris, J., 'Women and Episcopal Power', *New Blackfriars*, 53, pp.205-10, May 1972.

Russell, J., 'Violence and the Ulster schoolboy', *New Society*, pp.204-6, 26 July 1973.

Spencer, A., 'Politics and Religion in Ireland', *The Listener*, 88, pp.853-5, 21 December 1972.

'Try some old-time religion', *The Economist*, 245, pp.11-12, 30 December 1972.

Ballymurphy: A Tale of Two Surveys, Queen's University, Belfast 1973.

Whale, J., 'What kind of Ireland? Protestants who live in a ghetto of the mind', *The Sunday Times*, p.10, 30 January 1972.

'Is the bishops' rule being broken?' *The Sunday Times*, p.6, 23 January 1972.

6. Sects and Specialized Groups

Ballard, R., 'Family Organisation among the Sikhs in Britain', *New Community*, vol. 2, no. 1, pp.12-24, Winter 1972-3.
Barot, R., 'A Swaminarayan Sect as a Community', *New Community*, vol. 2, no. 1, pp.34-7, Winter 1972-3.
Chamberlin, E. R., 'With the millennium on their minds', *The Observer Magazine*, p.33, 25 March 1973.
Cotton, I., 'Festival of Light. The authentic voice of the British backlash?', *Nova*, pp.64-7, January 1972.
Douglas, M., 'Social determinants of belief studied in an English community of nuns', National Lending Library, Ref: HR727.
Harper, M., 'Charismatic renewal: a new ecumenism?', *One in Christ*, 10, no. 1, pp.59-65, 1973.
Harris, S., 'The Identity of Jews in an English City', *The Jewish Journal of Sociology*, vol. XIV, 1, pp.63-84, June 1972.
Hickman, B., 'A schism of isms', *The Guardian*, p.10, 19 August 1972.
Krausz, E., 'Anglo-Jewry: An Old Minority', *New Community*, vol. II, no. 2, pp.132-6, Spring 1973.
Metcalfe, R., 'Pick and shovel or social service?', *Friends Quarterly*, 17, pp.356-60, October 1972.
Nelson, G. K., 'The membership of a cult: the Spiritualists National Union', *Review of Religious Research*, vol. 13, no. 3, pp.170-7, Spring 1972.
Rigby, A., and Turner, B. S., 'Communes, Hippies et Religion secularisées', *Social Compass*, XX, 1, pp.5-18, 1973.
Turner, B. S., 'Belief, ritual and experience: the case of Methodism', *Social Compass*, 18, 2, pp.187-201, 1971.
Wallis, R., 'Dilemma of a moral crusade', *New Society*, pp.69-72, 13 July 1972.
  'Religious Sects and the Fear of Publicity', *New Society*, pp.545-7, 7 June 1973.

7. Religion and the Media

Gander, L. M., 'Where praise is due', *The Daily Telegraph*, p.13, 7 May 1973.
Guinan, M. D., 'Kung Fu: Violence and the Stranger in our midst', *The Christian Century*, pp.919-20, 19 September 1973.
Knight, P., 'Worship Happily Ever After', *The Daily Telegraph*, p.8, 21 February 1972.
Morris, C., 'Save us from religious TV', *The Observer Magazine*, p.9, 5 March 1972.
Stockwood, M., 'Godspell', *Records and Recording*, 15, p.8, May 1972.
  'Unholy Truce', *The Economist*, 243, p.28, 20 May 1972.
Wall, J. M., ' "Jesus Christ Superstar": A Surprising Film Success', *The Christian Century*, pp. 693-4, 27 June 1973.

8. RESEARCH IN PROGRESS

Addy, A. J., 'Some presuppositions about the nature of man and society in social work theory and social action', MA, Department of Social and Pastoral Theology, University of Manchester.

Atherton, J. P., 'Moral-theological aspects of the work of R. H. Tawney', MA, Department of Social and Pastoral Theology, University of Manchester.

Babb, G., 'The Theological-Ethics of H. Richard Niebuhr', MA, Department of Social and Pastoral Theology, University of Manchester.

Barraclough, D., 'A survey of training for the parochial ministry in the Church of England since 1800, with special reference to recent developments', FCP thesis.

Bonser, D., 'Issues for Christian Ethics arising from the working of the Abortion Act', MA, Department of Social and Pastoral Theology, University of Manchester.

Burton, L., 'The Social Stratification of two Methodist Churches in the Midlands in respect of Leadership, Membership and Adherence; a Study of the Social Structure of the Local Church', PhD thesis, LSE 1973.

Coles, D. J., 'The search for methods in contemporary ecumenical social ethics', PhD, Department of Social and Pastoral Theology, University of Manchester.

Dodds, A. H., 'Some modern theological concepts and their relation to group dynamics', MA, Department of Social and Pastoral Theology, University of Manchester.

Duncan, C. J., 'Judaeo-Christian and Marxist elements in certain Theologies of Revolution (with special reference to Martin Buber, Rubem Alves and the English Slant Group)', MA, Department of Social and Pastoral Theology, University of Manchester.

Finch, A., 'Religious Attitudes in the University – A Survey by Mail Questionnaire', Undergraduate dissertation, Hull 1973.

Hillyer, R., 'Twentieth-Century Parson's Wife', PhD in progress, King's College, London.

Hinings, C. R., 'The organisation structure of churches', Department of Industrial Administration, Aston University.

Ingyon, B. J., 'The Christian Socialism of William Temple and its subsequent development to the present day', (provisional) MA, Department of Social and Pastoral Theology, University of Manchester.

Maltz, D. N., 'Pentecostal churches in Edinburgh, Scotland', PhD thesis research, Department of Anthropology, University of California.

Maltz, R. B., 'Three evangelical churches (Adventist, Baptist, and Brethren) in Edinburgh, Scotland', PhD thesis research, Department of Anthropology, University of California.

Miskin, A. B., 'The influence of age and social classes etc. on church attendance in the Church of England', MPhil/PhD research in progress, University of Surrey.

Murphy, G. J., 'An elucidation and critique of the assumptions about the good society in contemporary case work literature', MA, Department Social and Pastoral Theology, University of Manchester.

Wallis, R., 'A Sociological analysis of a quasi-religious sect', Department of Sociology, Stirling University.